WINTER JOURNEY

A Play by

CLIFFORD ODETS

Produced in the United States of America
under the name of

THE COUNTRY GIRL

LONDON
SAMUEL FRENCH LIMITED

ISBN 978-0-573-01495-6
www.samuelfrench.co.uk
www.samuelfrench.com

FOR AMATEUR PRODUCTION ENQUIRIES

UNITED KINGDOM AND WORLD
EXCLUDING NORTH AMERICA
plays@samuelfrench.co.uk
020 7255 4302/01

Each title is subject to availability from Samuel French, depending upon country of performance.

WINTER JOURNEY

Presented by Henry Sherek and Sam Wanamaker at the St James's Theatre, London, on 3rd April 1952, with the following cast of characters:

(in the order of their appearance)

BERNIE DODD, stage director	*Sam Wanamaker*
LARRY, stage manager	*Guy Kingsley Poynter*
PHIL COOK, producer	*Robert Perceval*
PAUL UNGER, playwright	*Arthur Hill*
NANCY STODDARD, an actress	*Hazel Penwarden*
FRANK ELGIN, an actor	*Michael Redgrave*
GEORGIE ELGIN, Frank's wife	*Googie Withers*
RALPH, Frank's dresser	*Ian Main*

The play directed by Sam Wanamaker
Décor by Anthony Holland

SYNOPSIS OF SCENES

ACT I

ACT II

The action is contemporary

WINTER JOURNEY

Presented by Henry Sherek and Sam Wanamaker at the St James's Theatre, London, on 3rd April 1952, with the following cast of characters:

(in the order of their appearance)

BERNIE DODD, stage director	*Sam Wanamaker*
LARRY, stage manager	*Guy Kingsley Poynter*
PHIL COOK, producer	*Robert Perceval*
PAUL UNGER, playwright	*Arthur Hill*
NANCY STODDARD, an actress	*Hazel Penwarden*
FRANK ELGIN, an actor	*Michael Redgrave*
GEORGIE ELGIN, Frank's wife	*Googie Withers*
RALPH, Frank's dresser	*Ian Main*

The play directed by Sam Wanamaker
Décor by Anthony Holland

SYNOPSIS OF SCENES

ACT I

SCENE 1   The stage of a New York Theatre. Morning
SCENE 2   The Elgins' furnished room in mid-Manhattan. Later the same day
SCENE 3   The stage. Ten days later. Late at night
SCENE 4   The Elgins' room. A week later. Early morning
SCENE 5   A dressing-room in a Boston theatre. A week later. After midnight

ACT II

SCENE 1   The Boston dressing-room. A few nights later. After midnight
SCENE 2   The same. The following day. Early afternoon
SCENE 3   A dressing-room in a New York Theatre. Some weeks later. Evening

The action is contemporary

WINTER JOURNEY

ACT I

SCENE I

SCENE—*The stage of a New York Theatre. Morning.*
The stage is bare and disposed for rehearsal. There is a heavy iron door off R *leading to the dressing-rooms and stage door. The producer's table is set down* C *with three chairs* R, L, *and below it. There is a chair, and a table with a telephone on it up* L, *and a bench up* C. *The usual stage equipment, packs of scenery and spotlights, floods, etc., are stacked against the walls. An electrician's ladder stands at the back.*
(See the Ground Plan and Photograph of the Scene)

The CURTAIN *rises on a muted gloomy atmosphere. The stage is lit by a working light* C. *Soft radio music, a popular Mexican song, "Wayfaring Stranger," handled by a lamenting but insinuating tenor, can be heard off* R. BERNIE DODD, *the director, is perched on the upstage edge of the table* C, *facing* L *and softly whistling with the song.* BERNIE *can be very direct; he is small but with lots of wiry and graceful physical energy. At just thirty-five he is very successful, somewhat fretful and prowling when in rehearsal. Normally, however, his manner is friendly if a little watchful. From former excess of feeling about any and all things he has become saturnine and impassive in the face; there is a gloomy, thoughtful overtone about him. This gives him an air of unwillingness, as if he no longer wanted to be personally involved with persons or things; actually it is a form of protective distrust, expressing itself in what seems a main quality of being objective and impersonal, as if one were working with a screwdriver on a cold piece of machinery. But, of course, this mask of impersonality is not the truth.* PAUL UNGER, *the playwright, is seated in the chair below the table* C, *with his back to the audience. He is aged thirty, tender-hearted and open, simple in a good sense.* PHIL COOK, *the producer, is leaning on the chair* L *of the table* C *gravely and thoughtfully smoking a cigar. He is always gloomy, with a certain heavy pout about him, always dependent and uncertain of himself, but never wanting to admit it. It is very evident that the men have something on their minds. There is a pause.* COOK *scratches. Looking intently at Cook,* BERNIE *finally stops whistling.*

BERNIE (*to no-one in particular*) Where is that music coming from? (*He pauses, then rises*) Well, what about it?

(COOK's *face tightens and he will not reply.*
    LARRY, *the stage manager, enters* R *and crosses to Bernie*)

LARRY (*respectfully*) Do you want me to hold the company, Bernie? They're waiting.

BERNIE. Dismiss them. No. But tell them to stand by for a possible seven o'clock call tonight.

LARRY. Right. (*He turns to go*)

BERNIE (*to Larry*) Elgin, I want Elgin to wait.

LARRY (*stopping and turning*) Frank Elgin?

BERNIE. Yes, have him wait. Where's that music coming from?

LARRY. Prop man's room.

BERNIE. Oh.

(LARRY *exits* R)

(*To Cook*) Well, what's the verdict?

COOK (*in a low voice*) I wish I could lay myself away in a safety deposit box for a few months.

(BERNIE *snorts not impolitely.* UNGER *turns and represses a yawn*)

(*He looks painfully and resentfully at Bernie*) Bernie, you get the damndest ideas of any man I ever met.

BERNIE (*quietly*) I'm as annoyed as you are, Phil, but a little realism is of the essence, to quote one of your favourite lines.

COOK (*crossing below Bernie to* R *of him*) But what the heck's realistic about giving Elgin a reading? (*He crosses below Bernie to* L *of the table* C) Am I dumb?

(NANCY STODDARD, *a young ingénue, enters very timidly* R. *She is an actress, seventeen and virginal, which is to say untried and initiatory; but she has real if unfocused talent*)

Why not let the doorman read for the part?

BERNIE (*sternly*) Don't come in here, Nancy—we're busy.

NANCY. I'm awfully sorry, Mr Dodd. (*She moves to the bench up* C) I left my part on the bench. May I?

(BERNIE *nods impatiently and watches Nancy*)

(*She picks up her part from the bench, turns and crosses to* R) Please excuse me, everyone.

COOK (*fumingly*) Damn it, Bernie, I don't follow you and that's the truth.

(NANCY *exits* R)

BERNIE (*moving to* R *of Cook; coldly*) What don't you follow? We've been in rehearsal four days. (*Sarcastically*) Due to a technical fluke with the contract—not your fault, of course—Mr Billy Hertz, our leading man, is on his way to Hollywood and a flowery two picture deal. As of today, here and now, we are minus a leading man. Since we are booked into Boston on the twenty-eighth we are in trouble.

(*The music off ceases for a moment, then a new record "Am I Blue" commences*)

Cook (*impatiently*) I know all of this . . .

Bernie. Then let me read Elgin for the part. (*He crosses above the table* c *to* r *of it*) Twelve years ago I saw him give two performances that made my hair stand up. (*He turns abruptly and calls off* r) Close that door and keep it closed.

(*The stage door off* r *is heard to slam and the sound of the music ceases*)

(*He turns to Cook. Angrily*) Cookie, don't you understand? All I'm saying is let me read him for the part.

Paul (*rising; quietly*) That's right, Phil. (*He moves to* r *of the table*) It doesn't do any harm to give the man a reading.

Cook (*after a pause; shrugging his shoulders*) All right, read him, read him—I don't say don't read him. (*He sits in the chair below the table*)

(Bernie, *annoyed, prowls to* r)

Bernie. But don't make any cracks when I call him in.

Cook. But I happen to remember you looked this Elgin up five weeks ago for the part. He didn't do then and he won't do now.

Bernie (*crossing to* r *of Cook*) But I gave him the general understudy, didn't I?

Cook. Proving what?

Bernie. Proving I didn't think the whole future was behind him.

(Cook *mutters*)

What?

Cook. Nothing.

(Bernie *looks at Cook, then turns abruptly and moves* r)

Bernie (*calling*) Larry—Larry. (*He turns and moves above the table* c)

(Larry *enters* r)

(*To Larry*) Ask Frank Elgin to come in, kid.

(Larry *exits* r. Bernie *prowls up* c, *then turns and prowls* lc. *He crosses below the table* c *and leans against the proscenium arch* r. Cook, *disgusted, grinds his cigar underfoot.*)

FRANK ELGIN *enters* R. *He is followed on by* LARRY. FRANK *is an actor of fifty, whose present seediness does not hide a certain distinction of personality. He is nervous but nevertheless deports himself like the important actor he used to be. He stands there awkwardly, quite aware that three pairs of eyes are searching him.* PAUL *indicates Bernie with a nod.* LARRY *moves above the table* C. *As* FRANK *and* LARRY *enter the music off is heard and continues during the following speeches*)

FRANK. You want me, Mr Dodd?

BERNIE. Yeah, Frank, sit down a minute.

(FRANK *sits on the chair* R *of the table* C)

(*To Larry*) Company dismissed?

LARRY. Yes, sir.

BERNIE. Frank, I want you to do something for me. Not so much for me as for our producer and Mr Unger, the author. Read the part of Judge Murray for them.

FRANK. Billy Hertz *is* out for good, huh?

BERNIE (*ignoring Frank's remark*) Not that I can promise anything.

FRANK. Why do you want *me* to read?

COOK (*darkly*) Why does someone want you to read a part?

(FRANK *is puzzled and nervous*)

BERNIE (*turning abruptly and calling*) Hey, Props. Shut off that radio or close the door. (*He moves up* C)

(*The door off* R *is heard to slam and the music ceases abruptly*)

(*He moves and stands up* L *of Frank. Gently*) Read the part, Frank.

FRANK. Sure. All right. (*He rises but his attitude seems slow and reluctant*)

COOK (*annoyed*) Of course, you wouldn't take the part if we offered it to you, would you?

FRANK (*humbly*) I'm not fighting, Mr Cook. (*He takes a packet of cigarettes from his pocket*) If you want me to read for you . . . (*He takes a cigarette from the packet*)

LARRY. What do you want, Bernie?

BERNIE. The disclosure scene, end of Act Two. Find the place for him and wait outside, kid.

(LARRY *picks up a part from the table* C *and finds the place in it*)

COOK. Everyone in the theatre is slightly bats-in-the-belfry.

LARRY (*handing the part to Frank*) Don't want me to cue him in? (*He picks up a second part from the table*)

BERNIE (*taking the second part from Larry*) No, I'll do it.

(LARRY *crosses and exits* R. FRANK *takes a box of matches from his pocket and fumbles with it*)

(*He moves to Frank, takes the matches from him and lights Frank's cigarette*) Take it easy, Frank. I'm not looking for a performance. (*He returns the matches to Frank*) Sit, walk, anything you want.

(Frank *drops the matches.* Paul *picks up the box and returns it to Frank*)

Got the place?

(Paul *indicates the place in the script to Frank*)

Frank (*hefting the part in his hand; with attempted humour*) Yes. Feels like a Telephone Directory. (*He moves up* c)

Bernie. We can cut down to—Bert is already in—the Judge's line: "I didn't ask you to sit down . . ."

(Frank, *trying to hide his agitation, moves uneasily about up* c, *looking upward for the best light by which to read*)

Frank (*reading*) "I didn't ask you to sit down—because I don't want a louse on my furniture." (*He looks up*) That it?

Bernie (*sitting* l *of the table* c) Yes. (*He reads his part*) "I don't think this furniture will be yours much longer, Judge Murray."

Frank. "And I think I'll have to ask for an explanation of this big-mouth attitude. You damn Reform Party kids come and go like a ten cent piece of ice. Now get out before I kick you out! You only got in here because you know Ellen!"

Bernie (*bending forward and half rising*) "I resent that!"

Frank. "Not as much as I . . ." (*He moves nervously to Paul and points to the part*) What is that? I can't make it out.

(Cook *snorts*)

Oh! (*He reads*) "Not as much as I resent you, you little Wop bastard!"

Bernie. "I'm not letting you put this discussion on my personal plane. There's too much at stake!"

Frank
Bernie } (*together*) "I represent the collective will of thou——"

(Cook *sighs*)

Bernie (*rising*) No, that's my line, Frank.

Frank (*lamely*) Well, it's in this part. I can't see what I'm reading. I mean the light, I mean . . . Hertz is got the whole part pencilled up.

Bernie (*urgently*) Go on, don't stop.

Frank. I can't. I'm sorry. I'm saying, "Hands, behave!" but they're shaking like a leaf.

Bernie. Start right from where we left off. (*He reads*) "I represent the collective will . . ."

(Frank *looks at Bernie and Cook from under his eyebrows, not lifting his head, then he drops his eyes, slowly shakes his head, shuts his part and moves to R of the table up L)*

What's the matter?

FRANK. It won't do, Mr Dodd. I always was a dead bunny when it came to sight-reading. Thanks for the chance, but it won't do. *(He moves to the table C with bitter dignity, puts the part on it, and crosses to R)*

(COOK enjoys this part of the scene)

BERNIE *(to Paul; annoyed)* Give him a clean script, Paul.

(PAUL crosses to the table up L and picks up the script)

FRANK *(unhappily)* What's the use? You've been very nice, Dodd—you looked me up before—gave me the general understudy—I appreciate what you did, but . . .

(The door off is opened and the sound of music is heard)

BERNIE *(calling angrily)* Dammit, I want that door shut and stay shut. *(He tosses his script on to the table C)*

(The door off is shut and the music ceases abruptly)

(He crosses to Frank) I can't be that wrong, Frank—I know an actor when I see one. Let's forget the damn script. Let's improvise the scene. Just the situation—not the author's scene.

(BERNIE and PAUL move to the table C, pick it up and move it to R. PAUL then picks up the chair previously R of the table C, moves it R and sits. BERNIE flings the chair previously L of the table away to L)

FRANK. How do you mean?
BERNIE. Ad lib., just ad lib. it—improvise it.
FRANK. Look, Mr Dodd. I've never done that kind of Stanislavsky stuff.
BERNIE. Never mind. Come on, Cookie.

(COOK rises, picks up his chair, places it down R and sits)

(To Frank) Look at me! I'm a fresh kid—I wanna marry your grandchild and you don't want me to. That's the situation. *(He perches himself on the table up L. Acting angrily)* "I don't leave this house until I get your answer. Don't call in any servants or I'll knock them all on their ears."

FRANK *(moving about like an old man)* "Is—my daughter in the house? I have the greatest confidence in her. *(Scornfully)* Now I think I asked you to get out of here about a long moment ago." *(He moves to R of Bernie and glares at him)*

BERNIE *(after a pause)* That's it, Frank—that's the way you used to go. *(He glances triumphantly at Cook and Paul)*

(FRANK *continues the scene with strength and bitterness*)

FRANK. "Now get out of here! Don't look at me that way. Nobody wants your pity or your help. It's no satisfaction in a cold world to have your colder pity."

(BERNIE *rises, moves down* LC *and squats with his back to the audience*)

"Werba was a great man in his day—that's what all the loafers are saying. Werba made his millions, but the boy wonder is living with his in-laws now, they say. And now you come here and tell me, "Mr Werba, you're going to prison within the month." Well, let me tell you—Werba won't give up his name and take a number—Werba is still a great man. He tore an empire out of the world before he was thirty and he'll live to do it again. And when that time comes—you listen to this—I won't forget my enemies or my friends. I will never forget those who dragged me down."
(*He stops abruptly and sighs deeply, breaking a strange spell of majesty*)
BERNIE. That was the last speech of *Werba's Millions*, wasn't it?
FRANK (*moving to the table up* L *and leaning on it*) Yes. (*He rubs his hands and shakes his head as if dizzy. He gives the impression of slowly waking into a colder, shabbier world*) It came back to me.

(BERNIE *rises, glances briefly at Paul and Cook, then crosses to Frank*)

BERNIE (*gently*) Frank, would you wait outside for me? (*He leads* FRANK *to* R) Two minutes, in one of the dressing-rooms, please.
FRANK. Yes, I'll wait.

(FRANK *exits* R)

BERNIE (*crossing to* C; *repressing his satisfaction*) Well, what did you see?
PAUL (*rising and crossing to* R *of Bernie*) If you're asking me, something I wouldn't have believed. Where was that seedy guy hiding all that power and majesty?
COOK (*rising*) We've done three shows together—Bernie, I know you well. You're a man of violent preconceptions.
BERNIE. Didn't that scene speak for itself? (*He crosses to Cook*)
COOK. What did it speak? Does five minutes of ad lib. prove he can memorize and play eighty sides?

(PAUL *crosses and resumes his seat* R)

Just bear in mind this is for a potent seventy thousand bucks. He's been laying in pickle for a good ten years.
BERNIE (*quietly*) Someone took a chance one day with an actress named Laurette Taylor—and look what she did in her last few years.

Cook (*loudly*) But, darling, that man's a bleary bum! (*He moves up* c)

Bernie. Don't raise your voice—I don't want him to hear you. (*He moves to Cook. After a pause*) Well, what about him?

Cook. Look, you own twenty per cent of this show yourself. (*He crosses to Paul*) You're the playwright—doesn't this worry you?

Paul (*promptly*) Not if it doesn't worry Bernie.

(*Momentarily stymied,* Cook *hesitates then turns to Bernie*)

Cook (*quickly*) What about Ray Norton? He's still available.

Bernie (*sharply*) I don't want Ray Norton. He's my idea of nothing, just nothing.

Cook. Well, what do you think you can get out of *him*?

Bernie (*flatly*) I don't know.

Cook (*crossing to* R *of Bernie and facing him; aghast*) You don't know!

Bernie. How the hell should I know? (*He makes a mark in the air*) He's a big dark X! (*He prowls down* L) Do you think I underestimate the job if I use this lush?

Paul (*smiling to himself*) Don't raise your voice.

Bernie (*moving below the table up* L) We open in Boston in three weeks and two days. I'll have to manipulate and out-think him every inch of the way. (*He snorts*) Big comfort—my father was a drunk. I have some background for the job. (*He crosses to Paul*) But if this comes off you're apt to get something that happens once in twenty years.

Paul (*impressed*) I believe you if you say so.

Cook (*perching himself on the table up* L) And he's apt to have an ulcerated sponge for a brain, too.

Bernie (*crossing to* L *and turning*) We can stay out till he's letter perfect. The season's young.

Cook. But I'm not.

Bernie. Then what do you want to do? Postpone? (*He answers his own question*) Postpone!

Cook (*dismayed*) How can we postpone? We're in for a twenty thousand dollar bite already. The scenery's ordered, the guarantees on the house . . .

Bernie (*swiftly*) Then what do you want to do?

Cook (*after a pause*) Could we—look around for someone else while he's rehearsing?

Bernie (*firmly*) No, I won't do that. Once we start we don't let him go without real cause. A binge is real cause. Or if he can't retain lines. (*He pauses*) And, hold your hat, I wanna give him a run-of-the-play contract, not a two weeks' deal. (*Quickly*) Because I'd need his complete confidence, Cookie. Give him a two weeks' deal and he knows we can let him out any time.

Cook (*rising; indignantly*) No, sir! No run-of-the-play contract for Mr Elgin. (*He moves* R) I'd rather go back to Dallas, and . . .

(*The door off* R *is opened and the music is heard of* "*Sunny Side of the Street.*" Cook *turns to go.* Bernie *crosses quickly to Cook, takes him by the arm and turns him*)

Bernie (*quietly*) Okay, Phil—two weeks' deal.
Cook (*after a pause; disturbed*) What do we pay him?
Bernie. A coupla hundred a week.

(*There is a pause.* Cook *agrees by not answering and crosses down* l)

(*Warningly*) But I mean it, Phil—I don't let him out without real cause.
Cook. Umm.
Bernie (*to Paul*) Agreed with you, Paul?
Paul. Umm.

(*Poised, as if a dancer,* Bernie's *eyes and manner begin to sparkle; his attitude is tense but quietly expressive*)

Bernie. I'm one of those fools who saw Laurette Taylor in *The Glass Menagerie* eight times. Now—maybe something here—I'm not saying what—but it needs your real co-operation.

(Paul *rises, crosses to the bench up* c *and picks up his brief-case*)

(*He turns and calls off* R) Frank. Frank Elgin. Oh, Frank. (*He turns and prowls expectantly* c)

(Larry *enters* R)

Larry. You want Mr Elgin?
Bernie (*crossing to Larry*) Yes, send him in.
Larry. He's gone—he left.
Bernie. What do you mean—he left?
Larry. He left about five minutes ago.
Bernie (*impatiently*) Where? Coffee? What?
Larry. He just walked out, Bernie. He didn't say.

(Bernie's *face grows grim.* Cook *smirks at Bernie's back*)

Bernie. I see I'll have to go and get him.

(Bernie *pauses a moment, glowers then crosses and exits hurriedly* R)

Cook (*bitterly*) He's going to go and get him. (*He crosses to* R) In what Eighth Avenue bar?

Cook *wags his head, and exits* R. Paul *follows him off as—*

the Curtain *falls*

To face page 10—Winter Journey

Scene 2

Scene—*The Elgins' furnished room in mid-Manhattan, west of Eighth Avenue. Later the same day.*

It is a shabby, dark room. The door is R *and there is a small window up* LC. *A large double bed stands* R *of the window with small tables* R *and* L *of the head of it. There is a sink and dresser* L. *A wardrobe trunk stands in an alcove above the door. Below the door there is a small table on which stands a portable radio. An armchair and a dining chair complete the furniture.*

(See the Ground Plan and Photograph of the Scene)

When the Curtain *rises it is not possible to tell that it is high noon outside. Small wall brackets are lit, giving a feeble light. Loud music is coming from the radio.* Georgie Elgin, *Frank's wife, is obviously doing two things—suffering toothache, and standing* R *of the bed, packing a suitcase which is open on it. She is in her early thirties but looks younger, and is very attractive. Without her spectacles she is rather near-sighted. After a few moments there is a knock at the door.*

Georgie (*moving to the radio and calling*) Yes, yes, I'll turn it down. (*Instead she turns off the radio completely. Numb and listless, she moves to the bed, picks up a dress on a hanger and examines it*)

(*The knock on the door is repeated.* Georgie *glances at the door in surprise*)

(*After a pause*) Who is it?

Bernie (*off*) Is Mr Elgin in?

Georgie (*calling*) Just a minute. (*She moves quickly to the foot of the bed, picks up a blouse from the bed rail, puts it into the suitcase along with the dress, closes the case and pushes it under the bed. She quickly smooths out the top of the bed, then moves warily to the door and opens it*)

(Bernie *is standing outside the door*)

Yes?

Bernie. Is Mr Elgin in?

Georgie. No. I don't know when he'll be back.

Bernie. Are you Mrs Elgin?

(Georgie *nods*)

I wanted to talk to Frank.

Georgie. I don't know when he'll be back—he's rehearsing—in a show, you know.

Bernie (*pushing past Georgie; briskly*) I'll wait—it's important. (*He crosses to* c, *and looks around the room*)

(Georgie *looks rather stupidly at Bernie, and only when he looks at her does she seem to come-to with a start*)

Georgie (*crossing to the stove*) I was just going to make some coffee. (*She puts the percolator on the stove, looks vaguely at Bernie, wondering who he is, then attempts to make conversation*) Is it raining hard outside?

BERNIE (*leaning against the foot of the bed*) It isn't raining.

GEORGIE (*moving to the window sill and picking up the bottle of milk*) Isn't? Felt as if it were. It's cold out—the summer collapsed so abruptly, didn't it? (*She moves to the stove and continues making the coffee*) You could fall asleep here and not wake up till they called you for the Judgement Day.

BERNIE (*taking a notebook and pencil from his pocket*) What do I smell, incense? (*He makes some notes in the book*)

GEORGIE. It cuts the restaurant odours from down below.

BERNIE. I think I'd rather have the restaurant.

GEORGIE. It always comes in such spooky flavours, Sandalwood, Wisteria—this one's called Cobra.

BERNIE. I guess it's supposed to kill you. (*He snorts*)

(GEORGIE *smiles but abruptly winces*)

GEORGIE. Does my face look swollen?

BERNIE. No.

GEORGIE. I have a bad toothache. All of Autumn's in this tooth. (*She turns and moves to* L *of Bernie*) You don't look like one of Frank's friends.

BERNIE. I'm the director of the play he's working in.

GEORGIE. Oh! You're what's-his-name?

BERNIE. Bernie——

GEORGIE ⎫
BERNIE   ⎭ (*together*) Dodd.

GEORGIE (*after a pause; staring at Bernie*) You're even younger than I thought, from what I've read and heard.

BERNIE (*archly*) In this spot, most people would put in a flattering word.

GEORGIE. I amuse you, don't I?

BERNIE (*glancing impatiently at his watch*) No, but you act like an old lady and you're not.

GEORGIE (*moving to the window table and picking up the clock*) What time is it? (*She winds the clock*)

BERNIE. Twenty minutes to twelve.

GEORGIE. Three clocks, a radio—and never know the time. (*She turns*) Twenty after twelve?

BERNIE (*crossing down* R) Twenty *to* twelve. (*He looks at the photograph on the wall down* R)

(GEORGIE *sets the clock and replaces it on the table*)

(*He indicates the photograph*) That's a good photograph of Frank. Recent?

GEORGIE. Oh, a very long time ago—the year we were married. We went out to Hollywood that year.

BERNIE (*surprised*) Was Frank ever in pictures?

GEORGIE. For a year or two, but it was spooky.

(BERNIE *moves up* R *of the bed and looks at the photograph on the bedside table*)

People were endlessly kind, but it never worked out, and we came back. (*She indicates the photograph that Bernie holds. Sarcastically*) That's my father. I come from Hartford.

(BERNIE *moves below the bed, takes his cigarettes from his pocket and offers them to Georgie*)

No, I won't, thanks. (*She moves to the dresser, picks up a small bottle of hand lotion and rubs the lotion into her hands*) Isn't it strange—I thought it was raining. My hands are numb.

BERNIE (*lighting a cigarette for himself*) Does Frank usually come right home?

GEORGIE. Unless he sits out on the brown stone stoop. (*Abruptly*) Is something wrong?

BERNIE. Does Frank still drink?

GEORGIE (*with sudden alert evasion*) Just like us—one mouth and five fingers on every hand.

(BERNIE *looks archly at Georgie*)

What did you think I'd answer, Mr Dodd?

BERNIE. *Touché.*

GEORGIE (*replacing the bottle on the shelf; not hearing*) What?

BERNIE. *Touché.* That means . . .

GEORGIE (*interrupting*) Oh, come, everyone knows what *touché* means. (*She crosses to* R *of the bed and tidies it*)

BERNIE (*faintly annoyed*) What are we doing, jockeying for position? (*He moves to the window table and jabs a finger at the books*) Who reads these books?

GEORGIE (*coldly*) I borrow them on a library card.

BERNIE. Balzac, Dreiser, Jane Austen. (*He moves to the chair down* L *and sits. With a smile*) I'm afraid to ask you if you enjoy them—you'll bite my head off.

GEORGIE (*moving below the bed to* L *of it; intently*) I enjoy them. But I'd like to know what you're doing here. You're making me very nervous and I don't like it. What is this about Frank?

(FRANK *enters and stops abruptly when he sees Bernie. They stare at each other, a very direct man looking at a very indirect man.* GEORGIE *removes her spectacles and puts them on the window table*)

BERNIE. What happened to you?

FRANK (*removing his hat*) I decided to walk . . .

BERNIE. I asked you to wait.

FRANK (*after a pause; closing the door*) Any coffee, Georgie? Make some coffee. (*He puts his hat on the shelf* R)

(GEORGIE *crosses to the dresser, glances at the coffee pot, then looks at Frank*)

BERNIE (*rising*) I'm a busy man, Frank.

FRANK (*uneasily*) What do you want me to do?

BERNIE. Make up your mind—I want you to play that part.

GEORGIE. I'm an innocent bystander. Don't shoot me—just tell me what this is all about.

FRANK (*removing his coat and hanging it on the door*) Mr Dodd says he wants me to play the lead in his play. (*He takes a newspaper from his coat pocket*)

BERNIE (*briskly annoyed*) It's a starring part that needs an actor who can stay sober and learn lines. Are you that actor or not?

FRANK (*flaring*) Well, I'm not one of those goddam microphone actors, like Billy Hertz. I'm an actor.

(GEORGIE *fills two cups with coffee*)

BERNIE (*after a pause*) That's what I used to think.

FRANK (*evasively*) What about the producer? If looks would kill, I was dead.

BERNIE. He's afraid you're a drinker.

FRANK (*sullenly*) I don't drink on a show. (*He moves to L of the bed and sits on the downstage end of it*)

BERNIE (*sharply*) Not according to Gilbert. I checked with him—you worked with him in forty-four?

(GEORGIE *offers a cup of coffee to Bernie*)

(*He shakes his head at Georgie. To Frank*) What happened?

(GEORGIE *hands the coffee to Frank, then crosses below Bernie and sits in the chair down L*)

FRANK (*after a pause*) We lost our little daughter—that year.

BERNIE (*after a pause; quietly*) Can you stay on the wagon now?

FRANK (*after a pause*) Look, son, I think we oughta forget it.

BERNIE. Don't call me son. You've played bigger parts—you used to be a star.

FRANK (*gloomily*) Yeah, I used to drink a glass of money for breakfast, too.

BERNIE (*angrily*) What's the matter with you?

GEORGIE (*as if waking up*) You don't listen, Mr Dodd. Don't you see he's afraid of the responsibility?

BERNIE (*turning to Georgie*) But I'm willing to take a chance— the gamble's all on *my* side.

FRANK (*expostulating uneasily*) Why kid around? They open in Boston the twenty-eighth. I couldn't even learn the lines in that time. (*To Bernie; lapsing*) That part needs a Huston or a Barrymore.

BERNIE (*sardonically*) Bad enough to go to Hollywood to cast— now you suggest I go to heaven. (*He crosses to the door, turns, stares*

B

at them coldly for a moment, then speaks earnestly) Listen, Frank, you don't know me. But I was a kid when I saw you give two great performances in mediocre plays—*Proud People* and *Werba's Millions*. I can get the same show out of you right now—if you lay off the liquor. I have more confidence in you than you have in yourself.

GEORGIE (*sitting back and watching*) Why . . .?

BERNIE (*crossing to R of Georgie*) Because I saw him as a kid—I was a hat check boy in the Shubert Theatres. (*He turns to Frank*) You and Lunt and Walter Huston—you were my heroes. I know everything you did.

FRANK. Hear that, Georgie?

GEORGIE (*with quiet thoughtfulness*) Naturally, Mr Dodd, you exaggerate the sentiment to make your point.

(*There is a silence as* BERNIE *turns and looks very carefully at her*)

BERNIE. We killed the cat with sentiment? Okay, we'll bring him back to life with some antiseptic truth. I come from realistic people—I'm Italian. (*He pauses*) I'm not blind to Frank's condition—he's a bum. But I'm tough, not one of those nice "humane" people: they hand you a drink and a buck and that's exactly where they stop. (*He crosses to L of Frank*) I won't hand you a buck—but I'll think about you, if you take this job. I'll commit myself to you—we'll work and worry together—it's a marriage. And I'll make you work, if you take this job: *I'll be your will*. (*He pauses*) But if you do me dirt—only once—no pity, Frank. Not a drop of pity. Joke ending, kid. (*He crosses to R*)

(GEORGIE *looks more carefully at Bernie. We can almost see her come to life as she rises and takes a step or two towards* C)

GEORGIE. You'll be his "will"—I like that. That's what he needs, a will. And "no pity", I like that, too. I like the "antiseptic truth". But what kind of contract do you offer?

BERNIE (*promptly*) Standard two-week contract.

GEORGIE. Not run-of-the-play?

BERNIE. No.

GEORGIE. Doesn't that mean you could let Frank out any time with two weeks' notice?

BERNIE (*impatiently*) That's what it means.

GEORGIE. But suppose he takes the part and opens the show? He gets you over the top of the hill. How does he know you won't replace him?

BERNIE (*with flat indignation*) No run-of-the-play contract. Suppose we have to drop him? For drinking or for not retaining his lines? What do you want? Drop him, replace him and still pay his salary for the run of the show?

(*There is a silence as* GEORGIE *takes the cup from Frank and crosses to the dresser*)

GEORGIE (*presently*) I don't think he should take it. He needs confidence. (*She refills Frank's cup*) He won't have it with that two weeks' clause over his head. Would *you?*

(GEORGIE *has spiked Bernie's guns by presenting to him the same case he previously presented to Cook. There is a silence*)

BERNIE (*presently; looking from Frank to Georgie*) I have nothing in my mind except for Frank to play this part.

GEORGIE (*sharply*) That's sentiment again.

BERNIE (*moving* C; *heatedly*) I can't believe my ears. I came up here with the best intentions in the world—now I find I'm victimizing you.

FRANK (*rising; nervously*) May I get a word in edgewise?

BERNIE. What the hell did I do? Bring you a basket of snakes?

GEORGIE (*coldly*) *Noblesse oblige*, Mr Dodd. Stop whirling like a dervish.

FRANK (*moving to* L *of Bernie*) Nobody wants to get your goat, Mr Dodd. I—what I mean, Mr Dodd, it's only a matter of not wanting to bite off more than I can chew.

BERNIE (*after a pause; coldly*) You have the offer. We're booked into Boston for two weeks—(*he pauses*) but the season's young—we can stay out till you're letter perfect.

FRANK (*eagerly*) And—would you do that?

BERNIE (*promptly*) Do it? I *insist* upon it. Do I look green? (*He looks at Georgie*) I'll take that back—I am green. (*He turns to Frank*) Call me at the office by three o'clock. (*He moves to the door*)That means not later. (*He takes a twenty dollar bill from his pocket*) You need a twenty dollar bill? You need it.

(BERNIE *puts the bill on the top of the radio, then exits. There is a silence*)

GEORGIE (*presently*) Is that boy as talented as he throws himself around?

FRANK (*moodily*) Best average in both the leagues. (*He crosses to the dresser and picks up his coffee*)

GEORGIE. He's wilful, but he meant what he said.

FRANK (*moving down* L) I can't do it, can I?

GEORGIE. Doesn't it seem strange for you to ask me that?

FRANK (*unhappily*) You're my wife.

GEORGIE (*quietly*) Frank, we've been through all this before, many times before. (*She pauses*) I'm tired, Frank.

(FRANK, *brooding, does not look at her*)

FRANK (*crossing to the radio; murmuring*) What happened? Where did I get so bolloxed up? I was the best young leading man in this business, not a slouch.

GEORGIE (*moving and sitting in the chair down* L) Scripts didn't come.

FRANK. I knew it then—in Hollywood—I lost my nerve. And then, when we lost the money, in forty-three, after those lousy plays I produced . . . Theatre jobs . . .! (*He pauses, shakes his head, then takes the photograph from the wall and tosses it on to the bed*) This is the face that once turned down radio work. (*He paces to the window table and turns*) Whatever the hell I did, I don't know what. (*He moves to Georgie. Abruptly defiant*) But I'm good. I'm still good, baby, because I see what they think is good. (*He pauses*) Don't you think I'm good? *I* think I'm good.

GEORGIE (*quietly*) Then take the part. Make it your own responsibility, not mine—take the part.

(FRANK *looks at Georgie, and it is plain that the idea frightens him*)

Don't wiggle and caper, Frank. (*She rises. Suddenly*) Can't you admit to yourself you're a failure?

(FRANK *moves to the bed and lies on it*)

You'd die to save your face, not to fail in public—but I'm your wife; you have no face. Try to be clear about this offer—think.

FRANK (*after a pause*) I didn't hear him say he'd star me.

GEORGIE (*moving to the sink; with dry weariness*) I have a message for you, Frank: take the part. (*She commences to wash up*)

FRANK (*after a pause*) Yes, but what will *you* do if I . . .?

GEORGIE (*firmly*) Leave me out. Take the part and do your level best. (*She slowly moves a hand against her aching jaw*)

FRANK (*after a pause; uneasily*) But what about that two weeks' clause? You yourself tried . . .

GEORGIE. All I tried was to get a better deal. But you won't get perfect terms.

FRANK. You certainly gave him a scrap. (*He rises and stands* L *of the bed. Abruptly excited and cunning*) Georgie, I'll tell you. That two weeks' clause—they can give me notice any time, but *I* can give *them* notice too.

GEORGIE (*astounded*) But . . .

FRANK. Don't you see? They can let me out, but I can walk out any time I want. If I feel I'm breaking my neck . . .

GEORGIE. You can quit?

FRANK. Yeah, that's sort of what I mean, yeah. (*Bright and shrewd*) You see? Get it?

GEORGIE (*dubious and waiting*) Yes . . .

FRANK (*crossing to* R; *cunningly grand*) Why, with this two weeks' clause I don't even have to come into New York, do I? (*He moves to* L *of the bed and sits on the downstage end of it, chortling with glee*)

GEORGIE (*murmuring*) No. (*She moves down* L)

FRANK. That's the thing, that's it—two can play the same game.

(FRANK *is delighted at this discovery,* GEORGIE *much less so*)

(*He abruptly snaps his fingers and lights up even more*) Wait a minute. Quarter to seven this morning I had a dream. I laughed so hard it woke me up. That's a sign, Georgie, a hunch.

GEORGIE (*puzzled*) A dream?

FRANK (*seeing it*) A big sign—now get this—a big banner was stretched across the street: "Frank Elgin in . . ." I couldn't make out in what. Mayor La Guardia was in the dream—lots of people laughing and feeling good. (*He rises and crosses to Georgie*) I'm going to take that part, Georgie. You don't have to tell me not to drink—haven't I been a good boy all summer? (*Wagging around*) This morning I got up early—that funny laughing dream. And I was thinking about our lives—everything—and now this chance. Don't you see that all those people in the dream, they wish me luck. I won't fail this time. Because that's what counts—if the world is with you—and your wife. (*He looks at her, earnest, boyish and questioning, appealing for her support*)

GEORGIE (*after a pause; reluctantly*) I don't have any appointments—all winter.

FRANK (*excitedly*) That's what counts. I can't fail this time—I feel like Jack-A-Million. (*He gets his hat from the shelf and takes his coat from the hook*) I'll let Dodd know—I'll go up to the office in person. (*He picks up the twenty dollar bill*) But my first stop is the barber shop—I want the tonsorial works. Anything you want me to bring *you* back?

GEORGIE. No.

FRANK (*throwing her an extravagant kiss; really excited*) Catch that, dear.

(GEORGIE *catches the gift with an open hand.*

FRANK *exits. The door swings open.* GEORGIE *crosses to the door, shuts it, then switches on the radio. Alone, thinking, we see how unhappy* GEORGIE *is. Then she remembers her suitcase. She takes it from under the bed, opens it and looks unhappily down at its contents. She takes out the dress, then notices the photograph on the bed, picks it up and gazes at it*)

GEORGIE (*murmuring*) My God, my God, my God.

She drops the photograph on the bed and turns to hang up the dress as—

the CURTAIN *falls*

SCENE 3

SCENE—*The stage. Ten days later.*

When the CURTAIN *rises, the stage is set as before for rehearsal.* BERNIE *is seated with his back to the audience in the chair* R *of the table* C. LARRY *is seated in the chair above the table up* L. FRANK *and* NANCY *are standing* C, *rehearsing. It is late at night and the outer world has stopped for these working people; they have the quality of functioning fully, unaware of anything else.* FRANK *is working well, old muscles slowly coming to life, but he is worried about an inability to memorize his lines, although he will not say so. His part is rolled up in his hand.* NANCY *is letter perfect.*

FRANK. "No, no, no!"

NANCY. "You're taking all this much too seriously, Grandad. I'm going downstairs and let Bert in."

FRANK. "No, I tell you. I'm not going to see him, and you're not going to see him either—not tonight, not tomorrow—never."

NANCY. "Don't be silly, Grandad. I've been trying to tell you. We're going to get married."

FRANK. "You're what? Don't make me laugh! You don't know what you're talking about. You're still a child."

NANCY. "I'm eighteen, and I know what I'm talking about."

FRANK. "Ellen! (*He seizes her by the arm*) Now, come here and sit down."

BERNIE. Not so rough, Frank, not so rough. Take it easy—you'll break her arm.

FRANK. Oh. (*To Nancy*) Sorry, kid. Did I hurt you?

NANCY. That's O.K.

FRANK (*resuming*) "Now, come here and sit down. I may not have a very good reputation as a legal mind, but . . ." (*He breaks off*) Throw me a line, Larry.

LARRY. Oh—sorry, Mr Elgin. (*He prompts*) ". . . but I do happen to know a few little legal facts."

FRANK. ". . . very good reputation as a legal mind, but I do happen to know a few little legal facts, as, for instance—for instance . . ." (*To Larry*) What?

NANCY (*prompting*) "You're under age, you couldn't get a marriage licence."

LARRY. That's right.

FRANK (*to Nancy*) Never usurp the stage manager's position, dear. Older actors don't like it.

NANCY. I beg your pardon—I'm terribly sorry, Mr Elgin.

BERNIE. All right—let's go; let's go. We're hot.

FRANK. "You're under age, you couldn't get a marriage licence."

NANCY. "It's no use, Grandad. We've been over all this before and . . ."

FRANK. "Listen, Ellen, we can't talk to each other this way. I

can easily call to mind when you were—this high. You had a
funny habit. You said when you'd grow big, I'd grow small.
Children have that—(*he pauses; doubtfully*) delusion?" That's tricky
there, Bernie.

BERNIE. M'm.

FRANK (*hesitantly*) What does he mean?

BERNIE. First, a real psychological fact about kids. But the
theatrical meaning is more important. Show that he's trying to
win her over to his side.

FRANK (*after a pause*) But he isn't the kind who would openly
ask for sympathy.

BERNIE. Normally, no, but this is his only grandchild—his
defences are down.

(FRANK *thinks sombrely about this*)

NANCY (*timidly*) Do I know that he wants sympathy?

BERNIE (*rising and glancing at his watch*) No, Ellen doesn't
understand the situation yet. (*He crosses to* R) Now, it's almost
eleven o'clock.

LARRY (*with typical tact and deference*) I was just about to call
your attention to that.

BERNIE. Tell you what—let's send Nancy home. Our little
ingénue needs her beauty rest.

NANCY (*earnestly*) I'm not tired at all, truly I'm not. (*She moves
up* C, *picks up her coat and puts it on*)

BERNIE. Don't rush, child—life is long.

(FRANK *sits* L *of the table* C)

NANCY. Well, will you want me at ten tomorrow, then?

BERNIE (*ogling Nancy*) Why?

NANCY (*flustered*) Well, I mean I'm available whenever you
want me, night or day.

(*The men laugh*)

Oh, I didn't mean *that*. I can't bear it. I mean, I wanted to get
my hair washed tomorrow and . . .

BERNIE (*crossing to the table up* L) All right, come in at eleven.
(*He grins, picks up a script from the table, then he chases Nancy to* R)
And beat a hasty retreat right now, before I forget I'm a parent
myself. I eat little girls like you, without salt.

LARRY (*to Nancy*) Button up your coat and don't look so
flustered—we all adore you.

NANCY (*simpering*) You're very nasty, all of you, tonight. (*She
laughs*) Good night, everyone. Happy dreams.

ALL (*ad lib.*) Good night.

(NANCY, *happy and self-conscious, and full of young excitement,
exits* R)

LARRY. Off in a flurry of tender jingle bells—that's the age.

BERNIE (*moving below the table* C) Larryola, you don't have to hang around. (*He sits below the table and leafs through the script*)

LARRY (*rising*) Want me to switch on the pilot light?

BERNIE (*abstracted*) Yeah, sure.

(LARRY *crosses and exits* R)

FRANK (*after a pause*) Did I hear you say you were a parent?

(*The working light is switched on*)

BERNIE. I have a little girl of four.

(LARRY *enters, moves up* C, *picks up his coat and puts it on*)

FRANK. There's nothing quite like a little girl. Funny, I never got the impression you were married.

BERNIE. Neither did my wife. Five months ago she invented a phrase, "The Perennial Bachelor" and went to Reno to patent the invention. (*He indicates the script*) What about this damn hospital scene? You tired? (*He yawns*) Wanna stop?

FRANK. Well, I have a touch of headache . . .

BERNIE. Let's stop.

FRANK (*troubled*) No, let's go on. Judge Murray's character escapes me.

BERNIE. Well, let's chase him.

FRANK. Who's he like in real life? Hague, Hines . . .?

BERNIE. Any of those big political bosses. (*To Larry*) What's tomorrow morning's call?

LARRY (*moving to* R *of the table* C) Whole company at eleven. Except Mabel Beck—she's got that radio shot.

BERNIE. Scan the horizon, Larry. Come back if that little man is still outside. And kill that strip light. It's blinding me.

(LARRY *nods sympathetically, turns and exits* R)

(*After a pause. Pensively*) In my old age I'm ducking a man with a summons. Money—my wife wants money.

FRANK (*sympathetically*) Oh, no.

(*The batten is switched off. Real loneliness shows itself in* BERNIE, *but he now briskly pulls himself together*)

BERNIE. Let's talk about the character. How do *you* feel the Judge?

FRANK. Can I go wild? (*He rises. Intently, seeing and feeling something inwardly*) A bull—that's the image. Strong. Dangerous. On the alert; nothing shows though. A rigid face. A concrete slab for a face.

BERNIE. That's power.

FRANK. That's power—and pride.

BERNIE. Pride's a big colour to work for.

FRANK. Yes, he can't be wrong. (*He moves* L) Got everything he wants. Above the battle—withdrawn.(*His face narrow with thought, he begins to illustrate his words, and a ridiculous and cagey strut comes into his walk. In the rôle; murmuring*) I'm illiterate—why?

BERNIE. Because he's narrow, prejudiced, intolerant . . .

FRANK. But that's his strength.

BERNIE (*agreeing*) That's his strength—he goes narrow but deep—his own man.

FRANK (*in the rôle; excitedly*) I can do that—sure! (*He moves up* C, *then down* R) Now I know how this boy-o walks and talks. (*He crosses to* LC) That's in his way. (*Without a change of expression he sends the chair* L *of the table* C, *scuttling across the stage to* L *with one powerful and vicious kick. Imperturbably he struts* C *and drops back to himself*) Isn't that it?

BERNIE (*admiringly*) That's it.

FRANK (*eagerly*) But I have to like him, Bernie, even when he puts his wife away. Otherwise I can't get inside him.

BERNIE (*admiringly*) Where do you get these kind of feelings from?

FRANK (*moving up* C) I don't know. (*He picks up his coat, turns and circles a hand round his chest*) But when I get in here, inside—you can't get it technically.

BERNIE (*rising*) No, you're not a technical actor.

FRANK (*sighing*) Not many directors understood that about me.

(BERNIE *moves up* R, *picks up his coat, then moves to* R *of Frank and offers him a cigarette*)

BERNIE. Smoke?

(*There is a moody silence as both men light up their cigarettes and put on their coats*)

FRANK (*presently; glancing at his part*) I'm worried about the lines.

BERNIE (*perching himself on the table* C) Don't answer if you don't want to—how did a man with your talents go so haywire?

FRANK (*evasively*) That's a bow-wow with a very long tail.

BERNIE. What kind of woman is your wife? Just for chatter's sake.

FRANK. Georgie's got a very good mind.

BERNIE (*after a pause*) Then why didn't she want you to play this part?

FRANK. Was that your impression?

BERNIE. A yard wide.

FRANK (*evasively*) I don't know. She's on a hairspring, Georgie. Always has been—a hairspring. (*He nervously leafs through his part*) Sorry I don't know the words yet, Bernie. I wanted to surprise you tonight, but *non compos mentis*.

BERNIE. The sooner you get that second act out of your hands, the better. Why on a hairspring?

FRANK (*sitting* R *of the table* C; *uneasily*) It's like the hospital scene in the play. Where they tell the Judge his wife is—psychotic? What's the exact meaning of the word?

BERNIE. Insane.

(*There is a short silence as* FRANK *looks at his part*)

FRANK (*in a low voice*) The Judge, you see—isn't glad to get rid of his wife, the way the author says. It's very complicated. (*He clears his throat*) You tell an unhappily married man his wife is insane. He may feel relief, but at the same time he hopes it isn't true.

BERNIE (*keenly watching Frank*) That makes a richer scene.

FRANK. You can even say it's tender when he gets the news. There's so much to remember of living together—all the winters and summers, the times they were poor. (*His voice trembles*) And the fights, the snarling and yipping—settling blue murder with an hour in the bed.

BERNIE (*keenly*) Yes, if you played the scene that way . . .

FRANK. I'm not talking about the scene.

BERNIE. You're not?

FRANK (*fingering his part*) Georgie—was "Miss America" in the late thirties, the year I met her. She gave up a big career to marry me.

BERNIE (*delicately*) Is that according to Luke or Mark? You or her?

FRANK. Don't you believe me?

BERNIE. Sure, but what the hell is "Miss America" past twenty-five or thirty? What career? Marriage doesn't suit them any more—they don't want a home: the only piece of furniture they'll touch is the psycho-analyst's couch.

FRANK (*solemnly*) It cost me thousands.

BERNIE (*bitterly*) I had it for five years with the former Mrs Dodd.

FRANK. I bought a fourteen room house down in Great Neck the year we married. Never knew a better life. Swimming, boating, tennis, dinner at six—at seven she'd kiss me good-bye and I'd drive into town for my show. On matinée days she'd come in and we'd stay out late. Little spats and things, but it looked like a dream life to me. And then one night, I find her dead drunk across a bed—a kid who never took a real drink in her life. I didn't catch on that year—who could figure *that?* Career versus career— she didn't want me to play. Bernie, she was a hopeless drunkard inside a year. Then we had a child (*He pauses. Moved*) After that— every part I play, it's just like I ran off with another woman. I begin to drink myself. Don't ask me where the money went. She cuts her wrists, sets fire to a hotel suite—any time I'm on the stage she needs a nurse to watch her. And then, finally, we lost the child. You don't say, "Go to hell, good-bye", do you? By nineteen forty-four, forty-five—well, when you're in that situation you beat a bottle hard.

(*There is a silence.* BERNIE *pulls at an ear*)

BERNIE (*presently*) Does she still drink?
FRANK (*rising and smiling ruefully*) She stopped when I began. But I know how to handle her now—backwards, like a crab. About this part—to give you an instance—I had to make believe I didn't want this part. That leaves it open for her to convince me, her idea, not mine, see?
BERNIE (*rising; with a soft exclamation*) I guess you have to bring her up to Boston. (*He moves* L *of the table* C) I'm not against it. My wife was so twisted, "I hope your next play's a big flop", she says. "So the whole world can see I love you even if you're a failure." (*He turns to Frank*) As far as the work's concerned, I'm very pleased.
FRANK (*moving above the table* C; *eagerly*) You are?
BERNIE. You're a born actor, Frank—and this can mean the world to you.
FRANK (*solemnly*) I appreciate it, son.
BERNIE (*grinning*) And don't call me son again—I don't like it.

(FRANK *turns and moves* R)

(*He crosses to* L *of Frank*) Can your wife louse you up in this show?
FRANK (*turning and facing Bernie*) Don't worry, I can handle her. You know, you're a hot, gifted guy who got somewhere in a hurry. But you might be surprised in another ten years what you'll do for a little companionship.
BERNIE (*flatly*) No-one now living, under or over the earth, will ever again put me out on a tether.

(GEORGIE *enters* R)

I go wild when . . . (*He sees Georgie over Frank's shoulder, and stops abruptly*)

(FRANK *turns and looks at* GEORGIE. *From her reserved but pleasant manner neither man can tell what she has heard*)

FRANK (*quickly*) Georgie, what are you doing here? Where you coming from?
GEORGIE. From the movie show. Passing by—I thought you might be through.
FRANK. We were just breaking up.
BERNIE (*moving* C; *quietly*) Your timing was perfect—good evening, Mrs Elgin.
GEORGIE (*crossing to Bernie; smiling*) Yes, I have a knack that way. Good evening, Mr Dodd. How is my husband doing?

BERNIE. In my less than humble opinion, he's what they call a natural.

GEORGIE. Did I intrude?

FRANK ⎫ (together) ⎧Not at all, we were going to . . .
BERNIE ⎭   ⎩No, we were just closing . . .

GEORGIE. I don't like to make myself obtrusive when Frank is working. Unless he needs my help, of course. Am I in the way?

BERNIE (taking her measure) No, we were just closing up shop and giving it back to the theatre ghosts.

(GEORGIE, smiling vaguely, steps down to the footlights and looks over the auditorium. She stands there, unconscious of a kind of oriental posturing, consisting of a listening attitude, and a faint smile both polite and deprecating; she is her own aristocratic personage, unaware that a certain air of breeding never leaves her)

GEORGIE (softly) Nothing is quite so mysterious and silent as a dark and empty theatre—a night without a star.

(There is a short silence. FRANK and BERNIE look at each other)

BERNIE (crossing to L of Georgie) Why don't we go out for some coffee?

FRANK (moving to R of Georgie) Georgie? She makes all the decisions in our family.

BERNIE (very politely) Is that true, Mrs Elgin?

GEORGIE (archly) To the extent that Frank's brought out the mother in me, yes. I'd like some coffee. And I'd like to get to know Mr Dodd better.

BERNIE. And I'd like to get to know you better.

(FRANK puts a hand on GEORGIE's arm and commences to lead her R)

GEORGIE (looking into the auditorium) The theatre is mysterious.

BERNIE. That's true.

GEORGIE smiles at Bernie, then she and FRANK exit R. BERNIE looks reflectively after them for a moment, crosses, drops his cigarette end into a bucket R, then exits R as—

the CURTAIN falls

SCENE 4

SCENE—*The Elgins' room. A week later. Early morning.*

When the CURTAIN *rises, the window table is set for breakfast down* LC. *The bed is disarranged and the room has that untidy early-morning appearance. The radio is switched on.* FRANK, *without his shirt, jacket and tie, has just finished shaving at the sink. He is ebullient, in rare form, and completes his toilet as the scene progresses.* GEORGIE *is at the breakfast table, pouring coffee. She wears a wrap.*

FRANK (*drying his face*) Gonna get me some real expensive shaving lotion any minute now. (*He picks up the shaving mirror, crosses and hangs the mirror in the alcove*) Little things like that—the spice of life.

GEORGIE (*putting the percolator on the stove*) What?

FRANK (*raising his voice*) Shaving lotion, toots. (*He moves to the radio and switches it off*) I want some luxuries out of life. (*He takes the laundry parcel from the shelf* R, *puts it on the bed and opens it*)

GEORGIE. You talk like a courtesan, Frank.

FRANK. Then put me smack-dab in the middle of the courtesans if they like luxuries, too. (*He surveys the washing*) Boyo, I'll be glad to get away from this Chinese laundry. (*He shakes out a shirt*) The way they do shirts—it's a crime and a shame. (*He dons the shirt*) Looks like it was pressed by Dr Fu Manchu.

GEORGIE (*moving to the window and looking on the ledge for her spectacles*) Let's see—where would I be if I were a pair of glasses?

(FRANK *replaces the parcel of laundry on the shelf, then picks up Georgie's spectacles from the table* R *of the bed*)

FRANK (*handing the glasses to Georgie across the bed*) Right in my paws. (*He chortles*) See? You couldn't get along without me, Georgiana.

GEORGIE (*moving to the sink; smiling*) Someone's feeling mighty good today. (*She accidentally kicks over two empty beer bottles on the floor below the sink, turns and looks seriously at Frank*)

FRANK (*appealingly*) Put down that tomahawk. Didn't hide them, did I? Those two bottles of beer gave me a good night's sleep.

GEORGIE (*moving to* L *of the table*) When did you get them?

FRANK. After you fell asleep. I walked to the corner—got a *News* and a *Mirror,* the *Tribune* for you.

(GEORGIE *looks thoughtfully at* FRANK, *but he refuses to take her seriously*)

(*He crosses to* R *of the table*) Now, come on, Georgie, have a heart. I didn't hide the bottles and I got a good night's sleep.

GEORGIE (*sitting* L *of the table*) Are you worried about anything? (*She puts on her glasses, picks up the newspaper and commences to read*)

FRANK (*crossing to the alcove; readily, with a broad Italian accent*) Nothing is-a-worry me, except-a the lines. (*He picks up his tie and puts it on*)

GEORGIE (*quietly*) Don't start drinking beer, Frank. I'll get you some sleeping pills today. One a night can't hurt. (*She sips her coffee*)

FRANK (*looking at himself in the mirror*) Gosh, I'm getting baggy under the eyes. Sometimes I ask myself if it's me. (*To his reflection*) Hey, is that you, Frank? (*He replies to himself in a basso profundo voice*) Yesss. (*To Georgie*) Need a few ties, too, don't I?

GEORGIE. Wouldn't know where to start, you need so many things. Wait and see what happens.

FRANK. Yeah, we'll soon know. Oh, those critics. *Momma mia*, those critics!

GEORGIE. How are they up in Boston? (*She sips her coffee*)

FRANK (*dabbing his face with talcum powder*) Leave it to Poppa—he can charm a bird off a branch. No, ma'm, I'm not worried, not a thing. I'm taking it all in my stride. (*He tosses the towel on to the bed*) Oh, my, when I think of those great big fluffy bath towels in a good hotel. (*He picks up the newspaper from the table R of the bed*) We're gonna have fun, baby—you know that, don't you? (*He crosses to R of the table*) Wait'll I lock you in that hotel room.

GEORGIE. Drink your coffee, Rooster.

FRANK (*standing by the table and picking up his cup of coffee*) Yes, sir, everything is good and solid. It's Autumn again—I'm rehearsing a show—hear that? Let the wind blow down the street —the oysters and lobsters are delicious. (*He sips his coffee and finds it hot*) Hey, that's been near the fire.

GEORGIE. Look before you leap, silly.

FRANK (*grimacing*) My tie straight?

GEORGIE. Straight. Your shoes are being soled and heeled, the black ones. What else?

FRANK (*sitting R of the table; appealingly*) Blow on Frank's coffee for him.

(GEORGIE *smiles*)

(*He carefully sips his coffee, puts the cup on the table, then looks at his paper*) That's baseball for you. How do you like it—I'll miss every game of the whole series up in Boston.

GEORGIE (*after a pause*) Frank, does Bernie Dodd like me?

FRANK (*over-casually careful*) Why shouldn't the boy like you?

GEORGIE (*sincerely*) I don't know. Seems to be a chip on his shoulder. Does he like women?

FRANK (*innocently*) He's been married, divorced, has a child.

GEORGIE. I don't mind him not liking me, but shouldn't we face it realistically if it's true?

FRANK (*lightly*) See how it goes? Leave you alone for a few days and you get morbid.

GEORGIE (*patiently quiet*) Seriously, for your own sake, Frank. There's too much at stake. I don't want to be in your way.

FRANK (*abruptly, with edge*) Georgie, I'm winging like a lark—a million bucks couldn't compensate for this feeling of being back in harness. (*He commences to eat his breakfast*)

GEORGIE (*agreeing*) I haven't seen you with such zip in ten years.

FRANK. Then why make trouble, dear? When we get up to Boston I'm going . . .

GEORGIE (*quietly*) I'm not going up to Boston. (*She pauses*) My fine, womanly intuition tells me that Mr Dodd doesn't want me there.

FRANK (*angrily*) Yes, but I want you up in Boston. (*Wagging around*) That's all I need in this day and age—to leave my wife alone here, in a city full of wolves. (*He rises*)

GEORGIE (*soberly*) Are you jealous?

FRANK. What the hell are you talking about? Would I take this job without you? I *need* you up in Boston.

GEORGIE (*after a pause; simply*) If you need me up in Boston—that's most likely where I'll be.

FRANK (*interjecting*) Well, what are we talking about?

GEORGIE (*quickly*) That's enough, Frank—we've said enough. (*She rises, crosses to the recess and picks up Frank's jacket*) You'll be late.

(GEORGIE *moves to* FRANK *and assists him to put on the jacket*)

(*After a pause. With a smile*) You have a real conviction of woman's perfidy, don't you?

FRANK (*sullenly*) I thought we'd said enough.

GEORGIE (*crossing to* L *of the table*) I haven't felt like a woman in ten years. (*She sips her coffee*)

FRANK (*after a pause; sullenly*) I suppose that's my fault.

GEORGIE (*lightly*) Summer dies, Autumn comes, a fact of nature—nobody's fault.

FRANK (*indicating a button on his jacket*) Didn't you sew on this loose button?

(GEORGIE *moves to the cupboard under the sink, takes a needle and thread from the workbasket and looks back archly at Frank*)

GEORGIE. Spoiling for a fight, aren't you?

(FRANK *refuses an answer.* GEORGIE *crosses to* R *of the table, sits and deftly sews the button on the jacket*)

(*With serious lightness*) You mystify me, Frank, your sense of guilt and insecurity. Take a lesson from my father, the late Delaney the Great. He didn't care what people thought of him, no matter

what he did. Played every vaudeville house in the world. Didn't
show up at home but twice a year—and those two times he was
down in the cellar perfecting new magic tricks.

FRANK. Oh, sure, you'd love that—seeing me only twice a year.

GEORGIE (*whimsically*) My mother didn't mind it as much as
I did—it orphaned me. Might not have married you if I'd had
a father. But he believed in himself, I mean—you don't. (*She
bites off the thread*) That's cost you plenty——

(FRANK *moves above the table*)

—it's cost me as much.

FRANK (*after a pause*) You want me to beg you, don't you?

GEORGIE (*puzzled*) Beg me what?

FRANK. To come up to Boston.

GEORGIE (*rising*) I thought we'd settled that. (*She crosses to the
sink cupboard and replaces the needle and thread*)

(FRANK, *disgruntled, looks at his jacket*)

I pressed it last night. (*She sits L of the table and resumes her breakfast*)

FRANK. Where's that lousy part?

GEORGIE. In your topcoat pocket.

(FRANK *crosses to the door, laughs sheepishly, and takes his part
and a small address book from his overcoat pocket*)

FRANK. See, you can't live without me. But I don't know why
you talk that way—Winter, Summer—you're still a kid.

GEORGIE (*with a moue*) Oh, sure, of course, why not.

FRANK (*holding up the address book; teasingly*) Well, it's a small
world. Took her address—she's living up in Boston now. (*He
picks up his handkerchief and puts it in his pocket*) Susie Lewis from
Saratoga Springs. Our playwright's aunt no less—he brought her
around last night: haven't seen her in eighteen years.

GEORGIE. Attractive?

FRANK. Widowed and sitting on a mint.

GEORGIE (*smiling*) I'd investigate if I were you.

FRANK. Sue? She'd have me in a minute. (*He moves c and
displays himself, now fully dressed*) Well, am I decent?

GEORGIE (*nodding*) Say good morning to Bernardo the Great
for me.

FRANK (*taking his overcoat from the hook on the door*) You can bet
your sweet Fanny Maloney I won't tell him what you're calling
him. Don't you go tangling with him at the run-through tomorrow
night. (*He turns to the door*)

GEORGIE (*sharply*) Run-through?

FRANK (*turning; caught*) Now, don't tell me I didn't tell you
about it. I didn't tell you yesterday?

GEORGIE. Maybe you told Susie Peppermint or whatever her
name is. Don't you want me to come tomorrow night?

(FRANK *looks hesitantly at Georgie*)

(*Slightly irked*) Oh, come on, Frank, tell me what you want me to do. I won't love you less.

FRANK (*uneasily*) Don't feel offended, dear—I'd feel better if you didn't come. (*He crosses to* R *of the table*) This isn't a dress rehearsal—just a run-through with a few props. (*He pushes the chair into the table. Wryly*) They want the backers to see what they're getting for their dough.

GEORGIE (*easily*) Then I'll see it in Boston with the sets and the costumes.

FRANK (*fondly*) 'At's my girl! (*He crosses to* R) My only real worry is the lines—they won't stick in the dome.

GEORGIE (*rising and crossing to Frank*) Frank, don't get secretive. If I go on the road with you—tell me straight out anything that's on your mind. Don't shuffle—I don't often talk this way any more. We're both of us miles behind. Don't try to catch up all at once. We both know what's happened in the past. We'll have to live one day at a time, without resentments and evasions. We're at the bottom . . .

FRANK (*stoutly*) But we'll be at the top.

GEORGIE (*correcting him*) But—one rung at a time, separated by quiet healthy sleep.

FRANK (*squirming*) Yeah, you're right, dear, you're right.

GEORGIE. He's young, but he's a good man, that Dodd. Talk out all your worries with him.

(*There is a short silence.* GEORGIE *looks keenly at* FRANK, *who does not meet her gaze*)

FRANK (*presently*) I love you, Georgie. (*He moves to the door, turns and is about to throw her a defiant kiss*) Catch this one—it's a lulu. (*He changes his mind*) No, really get it.

FRANK *moves to* GEORGIE, *holds and kisses her, then turns and exits.* GEORGIE *smiles faintly to herself. After a moment, she goes to the table and, whistling softly to herself, takes some of the coffee things to the sink. The rhythm of her whistling slows down as she sees the beer bottles. She picks the bottles up, looks thoughtfully at them, then tosses them under the sink as—*

the CURTAIN *falls*

C

To face page 30—Winter Journey

Scene 5

SCENE—*Frank's dressing-room in a Boston theatre. A week later. After midnight.*

The room is small, shabby and untidy. The door is up L, and the window up C. Down R there is a chair, and a dressing table littered with make-up materials. A wash-basin is fixed to the wall above the dressing-table. A sofa stands under the window, and there is a chair LC. A tall cheval mirror stands below the door and Frank's wardrobe trunk, with a portable radio on the top, is standing open down L. Articles of clothing and costumes are hanging from hooks up C and overflowing from the trunk.

(See the Ground Plan and Photograph of the Scene)

When the CURTAIN *rises, the stage is empty but the lights are on. A first dress rehearsal has just been concluded out on the stage. The radio is playing softly. After a few moments* LARRY *looks in, sees the room is empty and is about to leave but changes his mind, crosses to the dressing-table, helps himself impatiently to a cigarette from the box on the table, then lights it.* PAUL *enters. He carries a script under one arm.*

PAUL (*fretfully*) Frank? (*He moves to* C) Where's Frank?

LARRY (*turning*) Looking for him myself.

PAUL. I have a few more cuts in scene four.

LARRY (*crossing to the door*) I'll take them later, if you don't mind. I'm trying to find out what happened in scene six. They keep blowing in the same spot.

PAUL (*following Larry to the door*) Six? I think the girl's throwing the wrong cue. Watch her when she walks down to the table.

LARRY. I don't know. Maybe . . . Frank cuts in there a moment too soon and . . .

*(*LARRY'S *voice dies away as he exits.* PAUL *follows him off. The voices of stagehands are heard off.*

After a few moments GEORGIE *enters. She is surprised to find the room empty. She wears her spectacles and is chewing gum. She puts her bag on the sofa, crosses to the dressing-table, blows her nose on a tissue, then tidies the table. She transfers the towel from the chair* R *to the wash-basin then picks up the shirt from the sofa, hangs it on the pegs, removes her own coat and hangs that on the pegs.*

BERNIE *enters)*

BERNIE. Where's Frank?

GEORGIE (*picking up the trousers from the chair* R) Isn't he out on stage? (*She hangs the trousers on the pegs*)

BERNIE. No. (*He sniffs*) Cobra?

GEORGIE (*smiling*) Wisteria.

*(*BERNIE *is about to exit, then stops and turns)*

BERNIE. Keeping in mind that it was a damn rough first dress rehearsal—the first time they've played in the sets—what did you think of the show?

GEORGIE. Oh, I didn't judge—just sat and listened to the words. But Frank looks wonderful, doesn't he? (*She removes the gum from her mouth, moves* R *and drops the gum into the waste-paper basket*) Chewed the flavour out of this two hours ago.

(BERNIE *and* GEORGIE *are each trying to get on a good footing with the other*)

BERNIE (*taking a packet of cigarettes from his pocket*) Smoke?

GEORGIE. Never use them.

BERNIE (*taking the last cigarette from the packet*) There's a whole pack since eight o'clock.

(GEORGIE *crosses to the trunk*)

(*He lights his cigarette*) These are really bad ones, these dress rehearsal nights. (*He crosses and drops the empty packet into the waste-paper basket*) Knock on wood—not one case real of nerves yet. The show's new to you, isn't it? What did you think of friend Frank?

GEORGIE. He was very tense, poor chick. (*She commences to tidy the contents of the trunk*) I'm fairly level-headed, making allowances for my sex, but I'd be in a blizzard, too, if my show were this ragged just before opening night.

BERNIE. But that's what two more dress rehearsals are for.

GEORGIE. You're as tense as a bug in June, aren't you?

BERNIE (*laughing*) Shh! Not so loud. My cast thinks I'm made of steel. Everyone looks for Poppa on an opening week, and I'm it.

GEORGIE. Frank thinks the sun rises and sets in you, Mr Dodd.

BERNIE (*carefully*) You'd make me very happy by being careful with Frank. You're his wife—he's probably all focused on your reaction.

GEORGIE. Is his performance pleasing you?

BERNIE. What do you think?

GEORGIE (*picking up the tie from the chair* LC) Don't ask me. I had one long old-fashioned cry out there. (*She hangs the tie on the hooks*) Just a country girl.

BERNIE (*crossing to* L *and leaning on the trunk*) Give him another week or two. He'll be very good.

GEORGIE (*thoughtfully*) But the show opens Wednesday night.

BERNIE (*reassuringly*) They'll get a show up here, but not what they'll get in New York.

GEORGIE. But what about Frank's notices here, on Thursday morning? You can't tell the Boston critics he'll be wonderful in *New York*.

BERNIE. That's the chance we take. Out of town try-outs mean education in public. You think Frank's that bad?

c*

GEORGIE. I think he's wonderful. (*Hesitantly*) But—I do wish I could follow the shape of what he's doing. (*She sits on the sofa, takes lipstick and a powder compact from her handbag and repairs her make-up*)

BERNIE. Too much detail, you mean?

GEORGIE (*carefully*) Yes, since you put it that way.

(BERNIE *paces to* R, *turns abruptly, crosses to Georgie, and speaks with a consciously used air of candour, like a politician*)

BERNIE. I think I can trust your intelligence, Mrs Elgin. Most actors don't need four weeks' rehearsing. They repeat the same glib, superficial patterns they found the first or second week. The usual actor gives himself small aims—or the director does it for him. In a couple of weeks they're fulfilled—and it all fits into a small, dull, peanut shell.

GEORGIE. And you think Frank . . .?

BERNIE (*humorously*) No peanut shell, he. His talent—the quality of it is improvisational. That's his blessing and his burden—he never knows what he is going to do next.

GEORGIE (*thoughtfully*) That's very keen of you to notice that. Many of his personal problems come from that.

BERNIE. He explores and discovers, as an actor, opening up the part very slowly. And my problem is to keep him going—overflowing. The longer I keep him fluid and open, the more gold we mine.

GEORGIE. You shut his talent off if you rein him in?

BERNIE (*nodding*) That's why I want him fluid for another week or two. (*He crosses to the door*) Let him flounder—in his case it's healthy. New York's five long weeks away. Don't mention any of this to Frank.

GEORGIE (*rising; stoutly*) I won't be that foolish, Mr Dodd.

BERNIE. I know you won't. Tell him I'll be right back.

(BERNIE *looks carefully at her, with a polite charm, masking a certain scorn. Despite her awareness of his good sense,* GEORGIE *is somewhat disturbed by him.*

BERNIE *turns and exits.* GEORGIE *moves down* L *and turns up the radio.*

FRANK *enters and closes the door behind him. He is an imposing and somewhat romantic figure, in evening clothes, a portly political boss with grey hair and moustache. He is nervous and tired.* GEORGIE *turns and looks at* FRANK, *who begins undressing, but with his attitude questioning*)

FRANK. I was upstairs, running lines with the kid. I blew like a bat all night. (*He removes his coat and hangs it up*) I hope this doesn't happen Wednesday, when we open. Well, what's the verdict?

(Georgie, *very moved, looks at Frank, momentarily not knowing how to grapple with his mood.* Frank *is afraid to hear what she will say*)

Georgie. Frank—you look wonderful.

(Frank *empties his trouser pockets and puts the contents on the dressing-table*)

I scarcely recognized you out there.

Frank. Was it bad?

Georgie (*gently*) Nothing was bad, dear. It was a bad rehearsal, of course. (*She sits on the chair* LC)

Frank (*disappointed and glum*) Yeah, I floundered like a fish, didn't I? (*He removes his waistcoat and tosses it on to the sofa*) What else did you see? I won't faint—you can tell me if I'm bad. (*He removes his tie*)

Georgie (*quietly*) I think you'll be astonishing in the part.

Frank. You don't look astonished to me. (*He removes his collar*

Georgie. Maybe I'm a little choked up, Frank.

(Frank *tosses his collar and tie on to the dressing-table and looks suspiciously at Georgie, not trusting her*)

You're keyed up and nervous. Be as unreasonable as you like.

Frank (*outraged*) Didn't you just see me act for the first time in seven years? Say hello, good-bye, or kiss my foot. (*He unbuttons his shirt and takes out his padding*) But don't sit there like Minne-ha-ha.

Georgie (*rising; trying to josh Frank out out of his mood*) I thought you were a little thick in the middle. (*She picks up the waistcoat from the sofa, and hangs it up*)

Frank (*muttering*) I need the portliness. (*He removes his shirt and tosses it at Georgie*) If I ever learn these lines, I'll call it Columbus Day. (*He cocks another suspicious eye at Georgie, lights a cigarette, then sits at the dressing-table and begins to remove his make-up*)

Georgie (*hanging up the shirt*) Frank, I don't . . . *You're* magnificent in this part. (*She stands behind Frank*) And the play—I'm deeply surprised that that quiet, smiling boy had so much talent.

Frank (*removing his wig*) Shut the radio off.

(Georgie *crosses and switches off the radio.* Frank *sniffs loudly, blows his nose and clears his throat*)

Georgie. Are you catching a cold?

Frank (*morosely*) That's all I need this week, a cold—I'd be a dead bunny for sure. You need more than a haircut to play this part—that's what I know.

(Georgie *picks up her handbag, takes a bottle of aspirins from it, and offers them to Frank*)

Georgie. Aspirins?

FRANK (*testily*) Give me a minute, dear. (*He bends down and unlaces his shoes in the same hurried rhythm which has blown him into the room. He stops abruptly and straightens up*)

GEORGIE (*fetching a glass of water from the basin*) What's the matter? (*She puts the water on the dressing-table*)

FRANK. Look at me going—zip, zip, zip! I can't even catch my breath. (*He removes his shoes*) Why don't they get me a dresser? Don't I deserve it? How can I make those fast changes by myself?

(GEORGIE *picks up the shoes, places them on the floor under the pegs, and puts Frank's street shoes beside his chair. She then gets his robe from the hooks and puts it around his shoulders*)

GEORGIE. Do you want me to speak to Mr Cook about it?

FRANK (*not looking at her*) Speak to Cook about it, Cook or Bernie. They can afford it with the salary I'm getting. (*He turns abruptly*) Do you know Mabel Beck gets more than I do? Three hundred a week and she stinks up every scene.

GEORGIE (*quietly*) She isn't bad in the part. (*She puts Frank's wig on the block*)

FRANK (*rising, putting his arms into his robe, and tying it*) That's right—stand up for everybody else. And look at that Nancy kid. Don't they learn stage deportment any more? Upstaged me twice tonight. (*He moves up* c, *acting it out*) Once I didn't even know where in the hell she was.

(GEORGIE *laughs soothingly.* FRANK *washes his hands and face at the basin*)

GEORGIE. Now, Frank, come on, take it easy. You'll have yourself believing all this nonsense before the week's out. First things first. Work well—that's your only concern.

FRANK (*promptly*) How'm I supposed to work with that damn understudy snooping around in the wings? Is that nonsense, too?

GEORGIE. Speak to Mr Dodd about it.

FRANK. You speak to him about it. (*He sits at the dressing-table and looks for the aspirins*) Tell him to keep the guy out front.

GEORGIE. What're you looking for? Aspirins? They're right under your nose.

FRANK. Yeah, but where's my nose?

(*He laughs sheepishly, ashamed of his bad humour; this breaks the tension between them. There is a knock at the door*)

(*He calls*) Come.

(PAUL *and* COOK *enter.* PAUL *carries a portable typewriter.* FRANK'S *manner changes immediately. Jovial, self-deprecating humour is the note, a protective masking, with nothing seeming to bother him*)

Welcome, gentry. (*He puts on his shoes*)

PAUL. Frank . . .

FRANK. Don't tell me about the show. I know—stank on rye bread.

PAUL (*sincerely*) Not to me. That hospital scene put a fine prickle on my skin.

FRANK. Don't kid the ugly man. (*Pleased*) Hear that, Georgie? The boy must like me.

(COOK *sits on the chair* LC)

PAUL. I like a good actor.

COOK (*to say something; gloomily*) Me, too.

(BERNIE *enters jauntily. He carries his script. There is a short pause*)

BERNIE (*to Cook*) Why's everyone so depressed?

FRANK (*jauntily*) Not me, I'm not depressed.

PAUL. Neither am I. I think the show's in swell shape.

COOK. Me, too, but it wasn't a very good dress rehearsal, was it?

BERNIE (*laughing heartily*) The worse damn dress rehearsal I've ever seen. (*He moves down* L *to the trunk, and leans on it*)

COOK. Then I fail to see the humour. I may be dense. Am I dense?

PAUL. I, if I may be excused, have a date with my typewriter and a pocket full of notes.

BERNIE. See you later, Paul.

PAUL (*moving to the door*) Fine. Good night, all you keepers of my integrity.

FRANK. Good night, Paul.

(PAUL *exits*)

Nice boy, one in a million. Not a speck of ego in him.

(LARRY *taps discreetly at the open door*)

LARRY. Excuse me, Frank—I have all the last scene people on stage. I'd like to run the spot where everyone blew—we can't locate what happened.

FRANK (*protestingly*) But I just ran it with the kid.

LARRY (*politely*) I'd be very obliged, Frank, if you'd run it again for me and the rest of the cast.

(FRANK, *with a mock groan, rises*)

FRANK (*executing a half dance step*) Oi, gentry, oi! (*He picks up his part*) Duty calls, but I'll be back.

(FRANK *and* LARRY *exit, leaving the door open*)

BERNIE. Frank's in high, good humour.

GEORGIE (*quietly*) Yes, he is. (*She sits on the chair* R)

COOK (*glumly*) Me, too, but don't ask me why. If he spoke one line of the author's script tonight, it never reached my ears.

BERNIE. Cookie, why do they open shows out of town?

COOK. Bernie, I'll never know. (*He pauses*) Will he know his lines for opening night?

BERNIE (*annoyed*) A little grey matter, Phil. (*He crosses to the dressing-table, takes a cigarette from the box and lights it*) He tripped on a rug he'd never seen before tonight. He couldn't find his slippers—his specs were in a drawer that wouldn't open, and a dozen other things. What do you want, miracles? Of course he dropped his lines.

COOK. I'm not worried. (*He rises*) Like the author—me, too— I beg to be excused.

GEORGIE. Mr Cook . . .

COOK. The stage hands are still out there on double time. (*He moves sulkily to the door*)

GEORGIE (*rising and crossing to Cook*) Mr Cook—do you think Frank needs a dresser?

COOK (*holding back his exasperation*) No, I don't. But I suppose you do.

BERNIE (*coming to Georgie's aid*) What does Frank think?

GEORGIE. Those two quick changes—it's a very large part, after all . . .

(BERNIE *makes a signal of assent behind Georgie's back*)

COOK. I know, Bernie—you think I eat shredded fifty dollar bills for salad.

(COOK *dolefully shakes his head and exits*)

BERNIE. Don't worry, we'll get him a dresser.

GEORGIE (*moving down* C) Mr Cook is almost what the bad fairy promised Frank at his cradle.

BERNIE. He's not that bad.

GEORGIE. I'm glad *we're* getting along, Mr Dodd.

BERNIE (*archly*) Did you think we wouldn't? (*He perches himself on the edge of the dressing-table*)

GEORGIE. You smoke too much. (*She pauses and moves* L) Who is that tall, gloomy man that lurks around backstage? Ford? Is that the name?

BERNIE (*agreeable but wary*) Yes. General understudy. Not much personality, but competent.

GEORGIE. Excuse me for saying this—must he stay backstage? It seems to bother Frank.

BERNIE (*after a pause*) I'll watch that. But is Frank that insecure? He's working well, in good humour all the time . . .

GEORGIE (*with a little friendly laugh*) Golly, don't you know he hides behind that humour? (*She moves to the door and leans on it*) He's not a simple man, Mr Dodd. That's why I offer myself as a sort of liaison officer between you both.

BERNIE. Is that what you're doing?

GEORGIE (*breaking*) I hope you don't misunderstand . . .

BERNIE. No, I think I understand.

GEORGIE (*after a pause*) Certain kinds of men, you know, are very strange. Business couldn't be better, wife and kiddies are fine. The next day you read he's hung himself from the chandelier. He can be the biggest kidder, too, it doesn't matter.

BERNIE (*solemnly*) Is that a picture of Frank?

GEORGIE (*carefully; a little afraid*) Yes and no. (*She pauses and moves to* L *of the chair* LC) He doesn't like to make the slightest remark that might lose him people's regard or affection. I've simply grown into the habit of doing it for him.

(*There is a short silence as* BERNIE *looks at her with a polite, regretful air*)

BERNIE (*rising and crossing to the chair* LC) I'm really sorry to say so, Mrs Elgin, but I hired an actor, a good actor. I may want him without his sisters and his cousins and his aunts. (*He sits, watching and testing her*)

(GEORGIE, *withdrawn, does not know what to say to this*)

What, for instance, bothers him now?

GEORGIE (*after a pause; plunging*) Mr Cook. His attitude. The ever-present understudy. The fact that he can't retain the lines. (*She crosses to* L *of the dressing-table*) He thinks he's not regarded highly enough to deserve a dresser. Salary, for another.

BERNIE. Why salary?

GEORGIE (*shrugging*) He's learned that Mabel Beck is earning more. In fairness to him, the figure is low for the part.

BERNIE (*archly*) The figure's fair. Not great, but fair.

GEORGIE. Granted, but not to him.

(*There is a short silence. They both are beginning to tighten*)

BERNIE. What was his last salary? And what year was it earned?

GEORGIE (*looking sharply at Bernie*) If you thought enough of Frank to give him the part—and you did—isn't that a very silly remark?

BERNIE (*coldly*) I happen to have other plans for Frank's financial participation in the show. If he works out—if the show runs—I make him a five per cent partner, as a gift.

GEORGIE (*crossing to* C; *hesitantly*) Would—you give him that in writing?

BERNIE (*rising angrily*) No, I won't give you that in writing.

GEORGIE (*pallidly*) It would help him if you did. Tomorrow—this week, staring probable bad reviews in the face.

BERNIE (*eyeing her*) You're clever—don't overplay your hand. Let's face it, Frank may go anywhere from here, even to a wealthy movie career. Or he may go right back to the gutter and you right with him.

GEORGIE (*after a pause*) Do you think that was called for?

BERNIE. Just like you, I don't always say and do what's "called for." (*He moves to the door*)

(GEORGIE *is puzzled, hurt, wary and trying to understand*)

GEORGIE. I don't mind you being angry—if I know why.

BERNIE (*flaring*) I have no problems with Frank—don't you make them where they don't exist. I could almost love a woman like you: my motto is "no pity," too.

GEORGIE. I wonder if you'd be kind enough to give me the code: what're you talking about? (*She turns, careful and restricted*)

(BERNIE, *invited as it were, crosses and stands behind Georgie, almost enjoying this moment*)

BERNIE. Here's the code. I'm ambitious—I wanna get my picture on a green postage stamp, too. There's a difference between us, of course. Way up on the twenty-fourth floor is where I live. And sometimes, late at night, I look out way over the sleeping city and think how I'd like to change the history of the world. I know I won't—the idea is talented but phoney. I admit I'm a gifted mountebank. What are you? Do you know? Do you admit it, even to yourself?

GEORGIE. What am I?

BERNIE. Lady, you ride that man like a broom—you're a bitch!

(GEORGIE *takes this with a slight gasp and roll*)

GEORGIE (*after a long pause*) You have a very lyric and lurid opinion of me.

BERNIE (*rapidly; in a low voice*) Now, be careful, Mrs E. It's a bitter mess for me if Frank fails. But I can hire other actors. I doubt if Frank can hire another director.

Georgie. I had no idea you were this tense tonight.

BERNIE. I'd tell you these same things any other night.

GEORGIE (*emphatically*) Yes, you would—you have the bloody eye of a man who smokes too much. Tobacco's a drug—it warps your judgement. I'll have to remember that.

BERNIE (*crossing to the door; sardonically*) I have to go stroke some more of my tender chicks.

(GEORGIE, *deeply hurt, stands proudly in helpless silence.*
FRANK *enters exuberantly and bumps into Bernie.* GEORGIE *breaks down* R)

FRANK. Shut my mouth, the traffic's bad tonight. Well, that spot's all cleaned up. Bernie, that line mixup—it was the kid's fault all the time.

BERNIE. Be back in two minutes—have to give Mabel Beck some notes. By the way, Frank, does it bother you to have the understudy hanging around?

FRANK (*heartily*) Me? Why in hell would a Ford bother a Rolls Royce? (*He crosses to the dressing-table and laughs*)

(BERNIE *cocks a quick smart eye at Georgie and exits, closing the door behind him.* GEORGIE *moves to the sofa, takes her handkerchief from her handbag, then moves down* L, *trying to hold back imperious tears.* FRANK *ripples on like a happy river, cleaning up and dressing quickly*)

Georgie, that line mixup—it was the kid's fault all the time. We'll get a load of fresh air in our lungs—I'll be dressed in a jiffy. How about a walk right across the Common? (*He hums a happy snatch of tune and continues to chatter happily*) Guess what I'm in the mood for? One of those one dozen oyster stews, half and half— just what the doctor ordered. Oh, boy, what that'll do for my stomach. (*He takes off his robe and tosses it on to the sofa*) What did that Cook say after I left?

(GEORGIE, *unable to speak, merely shakes her head*)

(*He half turns*) What? Huh?

GEORGIE (*with her back to him*) You're getting a dresser next week. (*She struggles to restrain her tears*)

FRANK (*practically exultant*) Really? Georgie, you beat the band! Can't live without me. I'll betcha Bernie was on my side.

GEORGIE. Yes.

FRANK. Look at me, just look at me—I'm winging like a lark.

GEORGIE (*half turning*) Frank—I wonder if I shouldn't go back to New York soon. You're getting a dresser now—and I think I'll be in the way. They resent me here and . . .

FRANK. What are you talking about? Are you kidding? Who resents you? (*He starts to move towards her; the lark is grounded now*)

(GEORGIE *turns her back to Frank, and abruptly bursts into tears.* FRANK *stops dead, baffled and frightened. Only slowly does he move to her with the shuffling gait of guilt*)

Why, darling—what's the matter? What is it, dear? (*He turns her and puts his arms around her*) Come on now, tell Poppa—what is it?

GEORGIE (*after a pause*) I really must—get these teeth fixed.

FRANK (*relieved; with fond and rough sympathy*) Honey, why don't you tell me when something's on your mind? We'll get you a good dentist in the morning. (*He crosses to the dressing-table*) Here, take some aspirin.

GEORGIE. No, I took a few.

(FRANK *turns, crosses to her, all sympathy, and about to kiss and embrace her*)

FRANK. Darling—don't you know this is gonna be a honeymoon, up here in Boston?

(GEORGIE *cannot help a bite of bitterness as she pulls away from him and sits* LC)

GEORGIE. Yes, we all love each other, don't we?

FRANK (*taken aback*) Boy, I'll never understand your moods, and that's the truth. A man can't be right, can he? Two strikes against him before he opens his mouth. (*Sullen and offended he crosses to the dressing-table*)

(GEORGIE *sits, stiff, cold and wordless*)

Now my stomach's all in a whirl again. That's what you wanted, isn't it? (*He sits at the dressing-table*)

(*There is a silence and distance between them*)

GEORGIE (*presently*) One day soon—we'll see what I want.

CURTAIN

ACT II

SCENE I

SCENE—*The Boston dressing-room. A few nights later. After midnight.*

When the CURTAIN *rises it is past one o'clock in the morning, a cold, depressing time. Photographs of the production are being taken out on the stage.* GEORGIE *is seated in the chair* LC. *She has her coat over her shoulders, is tired and depressed, but is covering it with a certain brightness and an excess of interest in what actually does not interest her. She is chewing gum, and knitting.* PAUL *has his typewriter open on the downstage end of the sofa and is sitting on the sofa, pecking away at the typewriter. The radio is playing softly.*

GEORGIE (*after a pause; looking up from her knitting*) I wish they'd get finished out there.

PAUL (*after a pause; hiding a yawn*) I've seen them take all night to photograph a show.

GEORGIE (*after a pause*) Uhh! I've dropped a stitch. (*Carefully*) Stitch, stitch . . . Makes me think of Hood's poem, *The Song of the Shirt.* (*She quotes*) "Work, work, work till your brain begins to swim. Work, work, work——"

PAUL (*completing the quotation*) "—till your eyes grow heavy and dim." (*He pauses*) You're very well read. I've noticed that before.

GEORGIE (*smiling*) What else could I do? My father was always away on tour, my mother was off with gardening and hobbies. (*She sighs*) I do wish they'd get finished out there.

PAUL. I've seen them take all night to photograph a show. Didn't I just say that? Groggy! (*He usually talks with a certain wry drollery and exaggeration because he is shy. Now he suppresses a yawn*)

GEORGIE (*suppressing a yawn and glancing at her watch*) Well, it's twenty after one. (*Musingly*) When you think about it—so many plays and books, so much reading in the stillness of the night— and for all of it, what?

(PAUL *stops typing and looks quizzically at Georgie*)

PAUL (*after a pause*) The moment I saw you, Mrs Elgin—the day I met you—I was touched.

GEORGIE (*with a moue*) Golly, you mean I'm touching?

PAUL. Tell me—why did Frank begin to drink?

Georgie. There's no one reason a man becomes a drinker. You should know that—you're a writer, Mr Unger. Looking back—I'd say bad judgement started him off. He had some money once, but you don't know my Frank—he wanted to be his own producer— eighty thousand went in fifteen months, most of it on two bad

41

shows. I didn't know a thing about it—he was afraid to tell me. A year later we lost our child—it was awesome how he went for the bottle—he just didn't stop after that. You know what the theatre is—give a dog a bad name . . .

(PAUL *yawns*)

PAUL (*quickly*) Excuse me, I didn't mean to yawn.

GEORGIE (*smiling*) Let's make a pact, Mr Unger—let's both yawn right out loud. (*She pauses. Impatiently*) Bernardo wasn't back tonight, was he?

PAUL. You don't like Bernie, do you?

GEORGIE. What's wrong with him? His wife?

PAUL. Among other things. But don't let that bluster fool you —he's actually a very innocent kid. (*He resumes his typing, stops and thinks, tries again, then finally stops*)

GEORGIE (*scoffingly*) Oh, sure, of course, why not. (*She rises, moves to the trunk and picks up the mug of coffee from it*)

PAUL. No, I mean it. Despite the talent, he's a dumb innocent kid in more ways than one. He's in love with art, for instance, and would make it a felony that you are not. But, as I say, there's more than popcorn in that head. Does my typing bother you?

GEORGIE. No. Does the music?

(PAUL *shakes his head, deciding to pack his belongings and go.* GEORGIE *sips her coffee*)

(*After a pause*) Frank should be in bed with his cold. (*She moves to the door*) What did you think of the opening last night? Were Frank's bad write-ups justified?

PAUL. Man is to man as the wolf—they were not.

GEORGIE (*moving to L of Paul; hesitantly*) Would you tell that to Frank? Make him feel good—he's low tonight.

PAUL. Sure I will. (*He massages a kink*)

GEORGIE .(*after a glance out of the open door*) Why do you work in a dressing-room?

PAUL. Frank's anxious about the new scene. And hotel rooms are very lonely.

GEORGIE (*crossing to R*) You're young to have found that out.

PAUL (*grinning*) As a friend, Mrs Elgin, that's a conceit with you—to talk like a veteran of all the wars. Actually, you're a young, very attractive woman.

(GEORGIE *moves to the basin, empties the dregs of her mug into it, then puts the mug on the ledge*)

As for me, I'll talk big. This is my third play. Loneliness is the badge of the writer's profession. It's ruined more good writers than every other reason combined.

GEORGIE. Am I as attractive as your aunt?

PAUL. Sue? She's almost as old as Frank. Very decent. My uncle left her cash, much cash. (*He closes his typewriter*)

GEORGIE (*moving to R of the sofa; delicately*) You could do something else for Frank. Ask her to have him out to lunch—it's a depressing week for him.

PAUL. Can do.

(FRANK *enters hurriedly. He has a bad head cold and is hiding a gnawing, nervous anxiety with affability and bluffness*)

FRANK (*crossing to the dressing-table*) How's that new scene going, sonny boy?

PAUL. I'll write you out of the play if that's all the respect I get.

FRANK. Well, two more scenes to photograph and we can walk. (*He looks around for the bottle of cough syrup*) Where's that cough syrup?

GEORGIE. It would bite you if it had teeth.

(FRANK *picks up the bottle from the dressing-table, takes a quick swig and looks around, as if bewildered*)

FRANK. Lemme see—what in hell do I wear next?

GEORGIE (*taking the smoking jacket from the hooks*) Just the smoking jacket.

(FRANK *takes off his jacket, hands it to* GEORGIE, *then takes the smoking jacket from her and puts it on.* GEORGIE *hangs the jacket on the hooks*)

FRANK (*crossing to the mirror*) Bernie hasn't been around yet? (*Quickly*) How about the new scene? (*He surveys himself in the mirror*)

PAUL. I won't get to bed till it's finished. Bernie wants to put it in tomorrow.

(*There is a short silence as* FRANK *thinks about this. He then moves to the trunk, takes a handkerchief from it, puts the handkerchief in his pocket, then bends and picks up a newspaper clipping*)

FRANK (*with a snort and a chuckle*) Yum yum! Did you see this notice? He claims I should have stayed retired. (*He replaces the cutting and takes a cigarette from his case*)

PAUL. Forget those notices, Frank—they don't mean a damn.

(FRANK *drops his cigarette*)

GEORGIE. Frank, don't smoke any more.

PAUL. How's your cold? (*He rises, puts on his coat, then picks up his briefcase and typewriter*)

FRANK (*grimacing*) Tutti-fruity!

GEORGIE (*sitting on the R end of the sofa*) I wish they'd get through out there.

PAUL. Intuition tells me to get back to the hotel—it's very close back here. (*He hefts the typewriter case*) It is generally supposed that I own this typewriter.

FRANK. Don't you?

PAUL. No, *it* owns *me*, body and soul—a form of depravity. Good night.

GEORGIE (*murmuring*) Good night.

FRANK. Good night, baby.

(PAUL *wearily drifts out*)

I like that boy. (*He crosses to the dressing-table*) Nice boy—not a speck of ego in him. (*He takes a cigarette from the box on the dressing-table, and lights it*) I have to have a cigarette, Georgie. I'm nervous. (*He picks up the bottle of cough syrup, his nerves and anxiety now showing through*)

GEORGIE (*after a pause; quietly*) I don't like that cough mixture you bought yourself.

FRANK. Why? It's a buck a bottle.

GEORGIE. A "buck a bottle" is a jim-dandy slogan, but you can read labels as well as the next one. Twenty-two per cent alcohol.

FRANK. Just leave it to me, dear. You know, Poppa—walks like a mountain goat—never slips.

GEORGIE. Let me straighten your tie, mountain goat.

(FRANK *replaces the bottle, crosses dutifully to Georgie and holds up his chin*)

You're naughty, Frank. (*She adjusts his tie*)

FRANK. You get some more sleeping pills?

GEORGIE. Yes. Don't twist.

FRANK. Red or yellow?

GEORGIE. Red, but all you get is one.

FRANK (*crossing to the mirror L and inspecting his tie*) How about the blue ones? I hear they *really* knock you down.

GEORGIE. Why don't we have a party some night? We'll start with the red ones in chicken broth. Then . . . (*She laughs lightly*)

FRANK (*sitting L of Georgie on the sofa*) Come here, Georgie. (*He abruptly takes her arms with a frightening intensity*) You're tired, too. Poppa's little helper. Go back to the hotel—we might be here another hour.

GEORGIE. I've waited this long . . .

FRANK (*rising*) Cook didn't come back, did he?

GEORGIE. No. (*She pauses*) Frank—what's the matter?

FRANK (*flaring*) Why in hell didn't Bernie come back tonight?

GEORGIE (*minimizingly*) Does he have to run back after every show to hold your hand?

FRANK (*crossing to the wash-basin and rinsing his hands*) This is only the second night, that's all. What're you saying—every show?

(*There is a silence during which* GEORGIE *carefully watches Frank*)

(*Slowly*) They wouldn't spend all that money taking photos, would they, if they were considering cast changes? (*Defiantly*) But I'm glad I got that two weeks' clause. (*He crosses to* L) And that's the truth.

GEORGIE. The pluperfect truth?

FRANK (*moving down* L; *bitterly*) The pluperfect truth! I'll hand in my notice. Why should I care—do they? Producer and Director don't come back the second night of a show.

GEORGIE (*quietly*) God is just where He was before.

FRANK (*turning sharply*) How do I know if I'm good? Can't you understand how I feel?

GEORGIE. Yes, I can. I think you're really agonized. But one thing is gospel, Frank: if you walk off *this* show, too, you'll never see me again.

FRANK (*with a step towards her*) Yes, ma'm, take their part—never mind what I'm feeling—take their part.

GEORGIE (*with quiet incisiveness*) This year I'm taking my own part.

(GEORGIE's *tone seems to frighten* FRANK. *He crosses to the dressing-table, sits and daubs at his face with a powder puff*)

FRANK (*after a pause; with a morose attempt at humour*) Why'd you ever marry me?

GEORGIE. That's easy: you always had a package of gum in your pocket.

(FRANK *snorts morosely, picks up some letters and reads one of them*)

FRANK. How do you like it? Fan mail—three of them—all jail bait. (*He reads*) "Have always wanted to be in the theatre. Am seventeen and think I have the talent." Jealous?

(GEORGIE *smiles*)

(*He tears up the letters and throws them into the waste-paper basket*) No, it wouldn't matter to you, would it, if I took out a gal?

(GEORGIE *smiles inscrutably. She knows Frank wants to recoup position, that actually he is trying to taunt her into a response of jealousy, affection and regard*)

Well, would it? Would you care if I didn't show up some night?

GEORGIE. I'm not exactly taking sealed bids, Frank.

(*There is a knock at the door*)

FRANK (*calling*) Yes?

(LARRY *enters*)

LARRY. We're ready, Frank, whenever you are.

FRANK (*rising*) I'll be right there, Larry. (*He picks up the bottle of cough syrup and slips it into his jacket pocket*)

(LARRY *nods and exits.* FRANK *sheepishly does not quite know what to say to Georgie*)

Wanna come out and watch them take a few of these archive specials? .

GEORGIE. No, it's cold out there.

FRANK (*crossing to Georgie; contritely*) Mad at Poppa?

(GEORGIE *shakes her head*)

Not even if we go back to the same life, same room?

GEORGIE. People don't go back to the same life, Frank. They go above it or below it, but they don't go back.

FRANK. But do I still have the country girl?

GEORGIE. Here I am.

FRANK. I appreciate you, dear. Don't wanna lose you. But I hope you know that if not for me, you'd still be on The Vine, in Hartford. (*He moves to the door*)

GEORGIE (*rising and moving to the dressing-table*) A toadstool in the woods. (*She picks up some tissues*) Here, take these tissues—(*she turns and moves* c) you'll need them.

(FRANK *moves to* L *of* GEORGIE. *They each hold on to an end of the tissue*)

FRANK. Thanks.

GEORGIE. And, Frank, leave the bottle here.

FRANK. I need it, dear.

GEORGIE (*quietly*) Over twenty-five years of know-how? Leave the bottle here.

FRANK. Georgie, I need it. (*Abruptly fierce but hushed*) I need it!

LARRY (*off; calling*) Everybody on stage for third act photographs.

(FRANK *jerks the tissues out of Georgie's hand, turns and exits. Alone,* GEORGIE *shows that she is tired; she stands shy, inward for the moment, head turned to one side, something very sad and lonely about her. After a few moments she crosses to the dressing-table and commences to tidy it.*

NANCY, *the flurried virgin, enters. Life is a long, delicious time to Nancy*)

NANCY. Mrs Elgin, may I use your pier glass a sec?

GEORGIE. Pier glass? Sure. Haven't heard that phrase since I was a girl.

(NANCY *postures at the glass.* GEORGIE *smiles*)

NANCY. Don't all people call this a pier glass?

GEORGIE. Only old ladies like me. Why, I go so far back I call rhubarb a "pie-plant."

NANCY. But you don't! I can't bear it.

GEORGIE. I do.

(NANCY *giggles as she examines her beautiful self*)

NANCY (*swirling around*) It's a beautiful dress, isn't it? My mother'll have kittens when she sees how low it's cut. (*She sighs*) Oh, Mrs Elgin, do you think I'll ever grow up? (*She moves* C) *Really* grow up?

GEORGIE. I know someone who wishes she hadn't.

NANCY (*moving to* L *of Georgie*) But you have no idea of what it means to be called "sweet child" or "Nancykins" by everyone and his brother.

GEORGIE (*dryly*) Yes, that can hurt.

NANCY. May I be forward? How old are you?

GEORGIE (*smiling*) On the dim, mysterious other side of thirty.

NANCY. That's old, isn't it? But look at you—(*she leads* GEORGIE *to the mirror*) come over to the mirror.

(*They put their arms around each other's waists and look in the mirror*)

We could be sisters.

GEORGIE (*after a pause; sadly*) Cherish your puppy fat, dear. It's a passport to the best of life.

LARRY (*off; calling*) Nancy Stoddard.

NANCY (*calling*) Here.

(LARRY *enters*)

LARRY (*slapping Nancy*) Hey, you're wanted on stage, Nancykins.

(LARRY *exits*)

NANCY. See what I mean? I can't bear it! Now you see why I'm so introvert.

(NANCY, *despairing, exits in a flurry.* GEORGIE *remains standing at the mirror; she takes off her spectacles and looks at herself; something poignant reaches out from image to reality. Soft waltz music comes through the radio.* GEORGIE *begins to sway to its rhythm, and in another moment, she waltzes alone down* R, *almost as if it were possible to waltz herself back to a better time. What she is murmuring to herself we cannot hear.*

BERNIE *enters and stands in the doorway.* GEORGIE *stops abruptly, routed*)

BERNIE (*leaning on the door jamb; sardonically*) Excuse me, the both of you. (*He comes into the room*)

GEORGIE (*moving to the dressing-table and putting a hand to her head*) Some aspirin—a headache. (*She searches for the aspirins*)

(BERNIE, *in silence, takes a bottle of aspirin from his pocket and extends it to Georgie.* GEORGIE *moves to the basin, runs some water into the glass, and takes an aspirin*)

BERNIE (*crossing to* RC) It's the Age of Aspirin, they say.

GEORGIE (*putting on her spectacles*) A splitting headache—too much stuffy dressing-room.

BERNIE. Where's Frank?

GEORGIE. On stage.

(BERNIE *turns and crosses to the door.* GEORGIE, *now in balance, stops him*)

(*She moves* C) His cold is getting worse, Mr Dodd. He shouldn't be kept up this late. It's more than flesh and blood can stand.

BERNIE. Them's melodramatic words. We need production pictures, don't we? How's his spirit?

GEORGIE. Low.

BERNIE. The show's in fair shape—why?

GEORGIE. Ask the Boston critics. Everyone doesn't have your confidence.

BERNIE (*promptly*) That's true.

GEORGIE. And while I'm on the subject, that confidence makes you push. That makes you a bit of a bully.

BERNIE (*even more promptly*) That's true, too.

GEORGIE. Don't minimize what I say by agreeing with me—it's really true.

(BERNIE, *tired, looks at Georgie with the typical curl of a smile, switches off the radio, then sits on the sofa, almost as if to bait her, a way of releasing his own present tensions*)

BERNIE (*after a pause*) What else is bothering friend Frank?

GEORGIE. You didn't come back after the show tonight. Neither did Mr Cook.

BERNIE. This last month I've spent from ten to fifteen hours a day with Frank. Nothing ever bothers him except through your mouth. Why?

GEORGIE. We've been through all of that before. (*She crosses abruptly to the door, closes it and turns*) He thinks it's a crime to lack a sense of humour. He doesn't want to be disliked. He hides when he's nervous. Either he jigs and jabbers away—or he sits in silence and rots away inside. But either way, for your edification, he's headed for a bender.

BERNIE (*mockingly*) Women always think they understand their men, don't they?

GEORGIE (*crossing to* RC; *quietly*) I won't fight with you, Mr Dodd. He expected you backstage tonight. Your absence was a reprimand. If you care at all for his sense of security . . .

BERNIE. Follow your advice?

(*There is a short silence.* GEORGIE *looks at Bernie as one wrestler looks at another*)

GEORGIE. Do you know anything about drinkers?

Bernie. Something.

Georgie. If you're not careful, you'll have him full of whisky before he goes to bed tonight. He's got a bad cold. That's a respectable surface reason for any drinker to jump down the well.

Bernie. Why work so hard at this marriage? Why not take a rest? You wear your husband down. You make him tense, uneasy—you don't stop "handling" him. You try to "handle" me, too.

Georgie (*in a flash*) And don't think I can't, after handling a cunning drunkard for ten years.

Bernie (*rising quickly*) Who the hell do you think you are? Secretary of State?

Georgie (*defiantly*) I'm a drunkard's wife.

Bernie (*snorting*) Girlie, I have to give you credit, but . . .

Georgie (*quickly*) No compliments, Mr Dodd.

Bernie. But I'm going to fight you as hard as I can for this man.

Georgie (*with a faint smile*) Not too hard—I may let you have him. (*She crosses to* r)

Bernie. No, you want him wholly dependent. Now let's not waste words. I . . .

Georgie (*moving down* r) Oh, it's much too late for that.

Bernie. I was married to one like you. Roughly, half my weight—ninety-seven pounds. It took her two years—she sewed me up.

Georgie (*dryly*) Love is hell.

Bernie (*moving to the door*) We'll leave it at that—joke ending. (*He turns*) What a bitter pity you don't realize the size of your husband's talent. (*He opens the door*)

Georgie. What have *you* given up for that talent?

Bernie (*moving* c) Then why do you stay?

Georgie. Because he's helpless.

Bernie. I'll help him.

Georgie (*moving to* r *of Bernie*) *You!* You wouldn't know where to begin. Life with him is three-quarters the avoidance of painful scenes. He's taught me to be a fish, to swim in any direction, including up, down and sideways. (*She crosses to* l *of Bernie*) Now, disregarding facts, you happen to think I wheedle his life away. You're very . . .

Bernie (*unable to contain himself*) Look, look, look! Half the world's shamed by sentiment. Say "mother" or "babe", "sacrifice" and they drip like axle grease. (*He crosses down* l) But you've ruined this man—don't explain it away by sentiment.

Georgie (*moving* c; *incredulously*) How did I so over-rate your intellect? You're a boy!

Bernie (*moving to* l *of Georgie*) Man or boy, I'm putting on a show—it has to work. (*He crosses to the door, then turns*) We can discuss universals some other day. To be frank, you are slightly grotesque to me, Mrs Elgin.

D

GEORGIE (*bitterly*) And what about yourself? Look at you, effective and hard-hitting—a machine, without manners or style—pretending to a humanity you never practise.

BERNIE (*moving to* L *of Georgie; contemptuously*) You called your own husband a cunning drunkard.

GEORGIE (*flatly*) It is necessary for you to know it.

(*There is a silence. They are murdering each other with their eyes*)

(*She crosses and sits* R) This is getting stupid. Now tell me, in God's name, exactly what you want me to do for Frank.

BERNIE (*pointing a finger at her*) That's fair! I'll believe everything you say: prove it.

GEORGIE. How?

BERNIE. Get out of town. (*He pauses and crosses to* L *of Georgie*) I've just had a bad fight in the box office with Cook. He's got a first-class replacement for Frank and seventy thousand dollars to protect. Frank will improve every day—I think he will—Cook thinks he won't. Well, he won't unless *you get out of town.*

GEORGIE (*after a thoughtful pause*) Umm! I'll do it. I'll go back to New York.

(BERNIE *turns and crosses to the door*)

But only on one condition.

(BERNIE *turns*)

Let me carefully tell Frank, in my own way, at my own time.

BERNIE (*crossing to Georgie*) As long as you're on the train by tomorrow night, understand?

GEORGIE (*nodding*) Life is earnest, life is real, and so are investments—I understand. But you may be sorry.

BERNIE. You're as phoney to me as an opera soprano.

(GEORGIE *rises, pushes her chair away and abruptly slaps Bernie across the face with her open hand*)

GEORGIE (*fiercely*) Did I forget to tell you I'm proud? Someone has to stop you from calling me any name that pops into your little head.

BERNIE (*frigidly*) Maybe I deserved that. Maybe not. Time alone will tell.

GEORGIE. It brings all things, they say. (*She holds back her tears*) Thank God for that inevitability.

(FRANK *enters*)

FRANK (*jovially*) Bernie, old boy, where have you been all night?

(BERNIE *crosses down* L)

Every time I come in here—you and my wife—what gives?

BERNIE (*with his back to Frank*) How they doing out there?

FRANK (*chortling*) We're through. Georgie, we're through—called it a day. (*To Bernie. Cautiously*) But, baby, did you see the show tonight?

(BERNIE *nods*)

Well, give!

BERNIE (*turning*) I'll tell you what a Harvard professor said—which is why I got back this late—"That man's extraordinary!"

FRANK (*crossing to the dressing-table*) Hear that, dear? (*He takes the bottle from his pocket and puts it on the table*) We're in the colleges now.

BERNIE. What happened there in act two again?

(FRANK *begins to change to street clothes. He removes the smoking jacket and hangs it on the pegs*)

FRANK. Bernie, it's that same damn thing, that same fast cue. Unger says it's all right to fix. (*He crosses to Bernie*)

BERNIE (*taking a notebook and pencil from his pocket*) I don't see why not. (*He makes a note*) I'd like to put the new scene in to-morrow.

FRANK. Tomorrow? (*He removes his collar and tie*)

BERNIE. You tired?

FRANK (*scoffingly*) Who? Elgin, the actor who likes to be compared? (*He tosses his collar and tie on to the sofa*)

BERNIE. Your energy was low again tonight.

FRANK (*unbuttoning his shirt*) Sure, it's this goddam cold.

(BERNIE *commences to test Frank. He is not stupid and there may be a modicum of truth in what* GEORGIE *has said. She stands up* R, *bracing herself, ready to have the truth out at any cost*)

BERNIE. Not nerves? (*Warningly*) We're gonna begin bearing down now. How *is* the cold?

FRANK. Under control.

GEORGIE (*to Frank*) Why don't you tell him what's bothering you?

FRANK (*rolling his eyes*) What's bothering me?

GEORGIE. Cook and the notices, for instance.

FRANK (*to Bernie; innocently*) I just wondered why he didn't come back, that's all. Is he mad? I mean, let's face it, they weren't exactly money notices. (*He sits on the sofa and removes his shoes*)

(GEORGIE *is not to be shaken off this time, despite Frank's tacit warning that she keep quiet.* BERNIE *watches carefully*)

GEORGIE (*moving* RC) Frank, Mr Dodd believes in you. I can't help you if you're worried—he can.

D2

FRANK (*very firmly*) But I'm not worried. He's got his own headaches, dear.

BERNIE (*with a step towards Frank; testing the situation*) Frank—you've talent—I expect to pay for that. I don't expect you to be easy and convenient—I'm no fool. Now, does anything seriously bother you?

FRANK (*rising*) Wouldn't I tell you if it did?

BERNIE (*still watching and probing*) I think you would.

GEORGIE. Did you or did you not tell me, ten minutes ago, right in this room, that you wanted to hand in your notice?

FRANK (*explosively*) Well, for crying out loud! (*He crosses to the dressing-table and sits*) If a man can't say anything in a gag . . . Have to watch my step—can't open my mouth no more. (*He throws Bernie a long-suffering look*)

(GEORGIE *purses her lips*, BERNIE *deliberately throws another chemical into the brew*)

BERNIE. Your wife says she's thinking of returning to New York.

GEORGIE. I told you nothing of the sort.

FRANK (*turning; alarmed and anxious*) What do you mean, New York? (*He picks up the cough syrup*)

GEORGIE (*deciding to take a new tack*) Yes—I might go back to New York.

(FRANK, *puzzled, worried, wary and off balance, is about to take a swig of the syrup*. GEORGIE *lifts the bottle out of his hand, bangs it down on to the dressing-table, then sits on the downstage end of the sofa*. BERNIE *crosses to the door, changes his mind, turns abruptly, crosses to the dressing-table and picks up the bottle*. FRANK *takes a cigarette from the box, forgets to light it, then starts cleaning off his make-up*)

BERNIE (*moving below Frank to* L) What is that?

FRANK (*minimizingly*) Cough syrup. Pine tar, cherries—a whole bush in a bottle.

BERNIE (*looking at the label on the bottle*) Do you know it's laced with twenty-two per cent alcohol? (*He replaces the bottle on the table*)

FRANK. Alcohol? (*He pretends surprise and puzzlement as he glances at the label. Glibly*) Yeah, there's alcohol in it, all right. I asked Georgie to get me some stuff to loosen me up in the chest and this is what she brought me back.

BERNIE (*sternly, but emotionalized*) What do you think you're doing, Frank? My father was a drinker—he ended up under subway wheels. I know what these little appetizers can do.

FRANK. Didn't even occur to me, Bernie. (*To Georgie. Chidingly*) Gee, dear, you wanna watch yourself on a thing like that.

(BERNIE *looks from Frank to Georgie*. GEORGIE *is tired but undaunted*)

GEORGIE (*rising*) Get dressed, Frank. I want to go home. I'll be waiting outside.

(GEORGIE *exits, closing the door behind her*)

BERNIE (*picking up the bottle of cough syrup*) Frank, my problem is the show. (*He prowls*) She's jealous of the show and jealous of me. (*He moves to the basin and empties the contents of the bottle into it*) This is how far she'd go—far enough to kick you off the wagon.

FRANK (*furtively and uneasily*) Bernie, I know she's high-strung and difficult——

(BERNIE *prowls down* R)

—but I can't believe she'd . . .

(*He breaks off as* BERNIE *stops him by clatteringly slamming the bottle into the waste-paper basket*)

BERNIE (*harshly*) I want her back in New York. We have hard work ahead. (*He pauses*) Frank, I wouldn't relish having to tell you . . . Go back to the hotel—get a good night's sleep. I want you fresh and clear—I'm putting the new scene in at one o'clock.

FRANK (*warily*) Yah.

(BERNIE *crosses to the door and opens it*)

BERNIE (*calling curtly*) Mrs Elgin.

(FRANK *looks uneasy.*
GEORGIE *enters, leaving the door open*)

BERNIE (*tiredly*) Frank knows exactly how I feel. See you at one tomorrow, Frank.

FRANK. Good night.

(BERNIE *exits, closing the door behind him.* GEORGIE *leans in silence against the door jamb. She is tired, worn thin, does not need much to make her break through.* FRANK, *full of childish guilt, does not know where to look. He chooses to begin by taking his make-up off, but he cannot look Georgie in the face*)

Where's my cigarette. (*He lights his cigarette*) He can be very arrogant and insulting, can't he? (*He pauses*) Must be cold out.

GEORGIE. Clean up, Frank. I'm beat out and in no mood to socialize.

FRANK (*switching out the dressing-table lights*) He had no right to talk to you that way. (*He rises*)

GEORGIE (*with some bitterness*) Did you tell him so?

FRANK (*moving to the wash-basin*) Georgie . . . He—I'm ashamed of myself. Give me two more minutes, dear. (*He washes his hands and face*)

GEORGIE (*eyeing him cannily*) Frank.

FRANK (*turning; innocently*) Yes?

GEORGIE. Where's the other bottle?

FRANK. What bottle?

GEORGIE. I'm tired, Frank—don't play peek-a-boo. Do you have another bottle of that syrup?

FRANK. No, I don't.

GEORGIE. Give it to me.

FRANK. But I didn't buy another bottle, dear.

(FRANK, *a twisted, punished child, stands looking at* GEORGIE *as she crosses to the dressing-table, searches on it, then pushes him out of the way and takes down the hat-box from the shelf. She looks in the box, then feels in the pockets of the garments hanging on the hooks*)

Wish you'd take my word for something for a change.

GEORGIE (*crossing to the trunk*) What a night, what a night. (*She looks in two drawers of the trunk*) And all the time there's been a clanging in my head—I don't know who's punishing who any more.

FRANK. I wish you'd take my word for a change.

GEORGIE (*abruptly*) Never mind. (*She puts on her coat*) I give up—I'm not going to look. Where's my knitting? (*She looks around, trying to locate both knitting and herself*)

FRANK (*confused, humble and abject*) Georgie, I wanna apologize, Georgie. He had no right to take that attitude.

GEORGIE (*collecting her handbag and knitting*) Didn't he? He has the right to take *any* attitude—in ten years he's the only friend you've had.

FRANK (*moving to* R *of Georgie*) Excepting you, dear. And that's what I want, dear, the chance to show you how much I love you.

GEORGIE (*frustrated and angry*) How much you *need* me, you mean. (*She moves to the door*)

(FRANK *is now revealed in all his naked helplessness and agony*)

FRANK. Please, Georgie, don't be mad at me. I know I'm no damn good, but I'm worried to death. (*He crosses to Georgie*)

GEORGIE (*moving down* L) Tell that to Bernardo.

FRANK. Think of what it means to me to walk out on that stage every night—the whole responsibility of the show is on my head.

GEORGIE. *Tell that to Bernardo.*

FRANK. Baby, I don't know where to hide—I'm ashamed. Don't know the old lines and tomorrow I get a big new scene. And now you say you're going back to New York—(*he moves to* R *of Georgie*) I can't do this if you don't help me. (*He pauses*) Did I ask them for this part? Didn't they come to me? Weren't you there when he came to me? They don't appreciate what I'm doing for them. They don't . . .

(GEORGIE *cuts him off intensely, changing his direction to one of heated indignation*)

GEORGIE. Stop putting on a front.

FRANK. Who's putting on a front?

GEORGIE. *You're* putting on a front. And you lie, you lie. (*She moves to the door*)

FRANK (*flaring*) What can I do, whine and complain? You want me to make them hate me?

GEORGIE (*bitterly*) They'll adore you when you go off on a bender.

FRANK (*moving RC*) Who says on a bender?

GEORGIE. Old waffle iron says. The mop behind the door. (*She moves LC, her eyes flooding despite herself*) This is how it ends—that laughing dream—you had a laughing dream, five weeks ago. (*She takes a handkerchief from her bag and uses it on her nose*)

(FRANK *turns away and changes his trousers*)

FRANK (*muttering*) I don't know anybody up here in Boston. The whole company—none of them like me, not even Bernie. How do I know he's keeping me on? Did he act like a friend tonight? (*He pauses*) Are you going back to New York?

GEORGIE. I don't know why not.

FRANK. You wanna leave me, don't you?

GEORGIE. It's late, Frank—I have to wash some stockings.

FRANK. Tell me. You do, don't you?

GEORGIE. I want to go to bed—I may have a happy dream.

FRANK. Who's in New York?

(GEORGIE *looks astounded*)

(*Harshly*) What pair of pants are you looking for?

GEORGIE (*outraged*) Frank, I warn you—(*she swings her handbag*) I'll hit you with the first thing I pick up.

(*There is a silence as they stand face to face, looking at each other for a moment.* FRANK *finally moves to the clothes hooks, gets his shirt and puts it on*)

FRANK. They all want me to fail. And you want me to fail, too. You don't love me.

GEORGIE (*wearily*) Come on, Frank.

FRANK. All I've got is two hands.

GEORGIE. Well, use them—it's two a.m. You have a one o'clock call.

FRANK. If you're in such a big hurry, there's the door. I, as a matter of fact, may take myself a walk. Get myself a baked apple and some milk.

GEORGIE. Your cold is getting worse.

FRANK. Let them worry about it. And I told you what you can do.

GEORGIE (*everything hurting*) You want me to go? Is that what you want?

FRANK. If you're in such a hurry.

(GEORGIE *looks at him and her face tightens. She picks up her knitting*)

GEORGIE (*angrily*) Oh, the hell with it! Just the hell with it! I'm going back to the hotel—do what you want. Sometimes I think you're plain out of your head.

(GEORGIE *exits without more ado, slamming the door behind her.* FRANK *glowers bitterly and snorts*)

FRANK (*circling the stage and mimicking Georgie's tone*) Out of your mind. Do what you want—plain out of your mind. (*He snatches up his tie*) Your cold is getting worse. (*He stands at the mirror L and ties his tie*) That's right—walk out on me. Typical! Typical! Forget I'm alive. Take their part and forget I'm alive. Helpmate, real helpmate . . . (*He dribbles off, his attitude abruptly changing. He listens for a moment at the door, then tiptoes to the trunk, takes a full bottle of cough syrup from the bottom drawer, uncaps the bottle and takes a swig. He bangs the bottle down on to the top of the trunk and adjusts his tie and collar. When he speaks his tone is less intense but bitter*) Helpmate! Sweetheart! Country girl!

CURTAIN

SCENE 2

SCENE—*The same. The following day. Early afternoon.*

When the CURTAIN *rises the dressing-room is in darkness.* FRANK *is lying on the sofa, asleep and snoring. He is fully clothed including his overcoat. There is a persistent knocking at the door.*

LARRY (*off*) Better get hold of Bernie—he went over to the hotel. (*He rattles the door*)

(FRANK *stirs*)

(*He calls*) Is there anybody in there? Mr Elgin. (*He knocks*)

(FRANK *wakes and sits up. He shows in everything the evidences of having been drunk until now, past two in the afternoon*)

(*He calls*) Are you in there, Mr Elgin?

(FRANK *totters to the dressing-table, switches on the lights and stands, blinking*)

(*He calls*) Frank?

(FRANK *realizes where he is and what is happening. The knocking ceases and a mumble of several voices in conference is heard off*)

FRANK (*muttering under his breath*) Oh, my God—my God!

(*He does not know what to do first. He tries to brush his hair back with nervous hands; nothing will help him at this moment, particularly as he is being hunted and pushed by further knocking on the door*)

COOK (*off*) Is the key in there with him?
LARRY (*off*) I dunno. (*He knocks then calls*) Is the key in there with you?
PAUL (*off*) Open up, Frank.

(FRANK *crosses to the door, kicking over a bottle on the floor as he does so. He looks around and realizes that he is trapped. He clears his throat*)

FRANK. Yes, yes—what is it? (*He pushes the bottle under the sofa with his foot, picks up his hat and hangs it on the hooks*)
LARRY (*off*) This is Larry, Mr Elgin. May I come in?
FRANK (*taking off his coat*) Yes, Larry, yes—just a moment, please. (*To himself*) Oh, my God! (*He hangs up his coat, but it slips to the floor. He shakes himself, dabs pitifully at his face and hair, crosses to the door, unlocks and opens it*)

(LARRY *and* COOK *are standing at the door, with* PAUL *behind them*)

What's wrong? (*He turns and crosses to* RC) What's wrong, boys?

(LARRY *enters and stands* C. PAUL *enters and moves to* L *of Larry.* COOK *enters and stands* L)

LARRY. It's past two o'clock, Mr Elgin.

FRANK (*blustering with a crooked smile*) Well, where's the fire?

LARRY. Your door was locked and the key wasn't on the rack.

FRANK. I was napping in here. Tired. (*He moves to the dressing-table, takes a cigarette from the box, but his hands shake so that he is unable to light it*)

COOK (*moving to* L *of Larry*) There was a one o'clock call, for the new scene.

FRANK. Oh God! Completely slipped my mind.

(COOK *breaks down* L)

Walked around. Got tired and slept in here and just forgot.

(LARRY *lights Frank's cigarette*)

COOK. You mean you "slept it off" in here. You're so loaded you can't stand straight right now.

(FRANK *sits* R)

What the dickens happened to you?

LARRY (*restrainingly*) Mr Cook . . .

FRANK (*snarling*) Nothing happened to me. I have a cold. Had a couple of beers and some food. (*He puts his head in his hands; the world is whirling for him*)

COOK		(*He paces up and down* L) Look at him! Smells like the sovereign state of Kentucky in person.
	(*together*)	
PAUL		Where's Bernie?
LARRY		We've sent for him.

(GEORGIE *enters. Only* LARRY *sees her*)

COOK (*fervidly*) Well, this does it! Thank my lucky stars this does it. That wife of yours can help you start packing. (*He crosses towards Frank*)

(PAUL *restrains* COOK, *takes him by the arm and leads him down* L)

LARRY. Mr Cook, I can't let you talk to an actor that way.

COOK (*not believing his ears*) You can't what?

LARRY (*white-faced*) You're the boss, Mr Cook, but you can't talk that way to an actor in any show I'm on. I won't permit it.

COOK. *You* won't permit it?

LARRY. There is a lady in the room, too. I'll have to ask you to keep quiet until Bernie gets here.

COOK (*grimly*) We'll see what he says when *he* gets here.

(COOK *exits.* PAUL *shakes his head dolefully at Georgie and follows Cook off.* FRANK *does not look up. There is a short silence, then* LARRY *crosses to Frank*)

LARRY (*kindly*) Can I get you some coffee, Frank?

(FRANK *does not answer or lift his head*)

GEORGIE. Don't get him coffee, Larry—it makes him sicker.

LARRY (*after a pause*) I'll get you an alka-seltzer.

(LARRY *looks at Georgie, crosses and exits, closing the door behind him*)

GEORGIE. Where were you all night?

(FRANK *rises, reels to the sofa and falls on to it in a sitting position*)

FRANK (*with averted eyes*) Get me some water.

(GEORGIE *crosses, puts her bag on the dressing-table, then moves to the basin and turns on the water*)

GEORGIE. It's not very cold.

FRANK. Let it run. (*He pauses*) Where's Bernie?

GEORGIE. I dunno. Watch that cigarette, Frank. (*She fills a glass with water*) You'll have us all on fire in a minute.

(FRANK *drops the cigarette underfoot and grinds it dead*)

FRANK (*bitterly*) I missed the reading and that's all I did miss.

(GEORGIE *crosses and hands the glass of water to Frank.*
BERNIE *enters and switches on the room lights.* COOK *and* PAUL *follow Bernie on.* FRANK *drops his eyes and his soul drops its head within.* BERNIE *crosses to* C, *turns squarely on a line with Georgie and speaks in a low but tense voice*)

BERNIE. When did you see your husband last, Mrs Elgin?

GEORGIE (*looking warily at Bernie*) Past two this morning.

BERNIE. Where?

GEORGIE. In this room.

BERNIE. Did he go back to the hotel with you?

GEORGIE. No, he wanted to go for food. I was tired.

BERNIE. What did you tell me when I phoned you in your room today?

GEORGIE. You asked me where Frank was. I said I didn't know. You asked me if he'd had a good night's sleep. I hoped he had, I said.

BERNIE. Why did you lie?

(*This scene is so painful to* PAUL *that he exits quietly, closing the door behind him*)

GEORGIE. I am not aware, Mr Dodd, that I lied.

BERNIE. You didn't think it was important to tell me that Frank hadn't been home all night?

GEORGIE. Suppose he'd been with another woman?

BERNIE. You're being deliberately evasive and childish.

(*There is a tap at the door*)

LARRY (*off*) It's Larry.

BERNIE (*barking*) Wait outside. (*To Georgie*) Where did you get him a bottle after midnight?

GEORGIE. Where did I . . .? (*She is so astounded that she is unable to resist a strange, strained laugh*)

COOK. What the heck's so funny? I resent that!

BERNIE (*turning to Cook*) There's only one thing to do, Phil . . .

COOK. And, yes sir, I'm going right out to the box office to do it.

(COOK *exits, slamming the door behind him. There is a short silence*)

BERNIE (*without looking at Georgie*) There is still one person too many in this room.

(GEORGIE *smiles faintly, then crosses and exits, closing the door behind her. She does not take her handbag. We do not know what* BERNIE *is going to do, but now he breaks a momentary silence*)

(*Quietly*) What about this?

(FRANK, *head down, does not answer.* BERNIE *waits; and then we see that he is really very emotional about this incident, for now his voice vibrates when he speaks*)

I'm in a mood to cut my throat in public. God A'mighty, human beings are funny people. (*He pauses. Abruptly harsh*) Sit up! Don't act as if I'm beating you up. Don't make me the victimizer. Sit up! (*It seems for a moment that he may hit Frank; instead he turns and breaks* L)

FRANK (*after a pause*) Don't bawl me out, Bernie. I'll stay till you get somebody else.

BERNIE. I'm tired right down to my bones. (*Strongly*) That wife of yours—she . . .

FRANK (*hopelessly*) No, not my wife. Why kid around? It's all my fault—I'm no good.

BERNIE (*briskly*) You're guilty as hell! But I want you to do something for the kid.

FRANK. What kid?

BERNIE. *This* kid. Stop being naïve: stop protecting her.

FRANK. Bernie, she's weak. She . . .

BERNIE. She's driven you to drink for ten years and you call her weak? You might be magnificent in this part, but it would have to start with her. She goes back to New York on the *Five-o-Five*.

FRANK (*weakly*) Bernie, kid, I can't leave her. Left her once—she cut her wrists. She'd cut her wrists again.

BERNIE (*angrily*) She goes back today.

FRANK (*in a nervous whisper*) Bernie, she's weak.

BERNIE. I'll talk to her. *If* we go on together, you move in with me for the duration. (*He moves to the door*)

FRANK (*rising*) But Mr Cook—he doesn't want me and . . .

BERNIE (*flashing*) I'm not so sure I want you. (*He opens the door and calls crisply*) Mrs Elgin.

FRANK (*resuming his seat on the sofa; fumblingly*) Bernie, you decide . . .

(GEORGIE *enters. She carries a glass of alka-seltzer. She closes the door, crosses to Frank and hands him the drink*)

GEORGIE. Take this.

(FRANK *takes the glass but does not drink.* BERNIE *moves down* L)

BERNIE. Frank stays—you go.

(GEORGIE *turns to Bernie, a wary hatred in her eyes*)

The management will take care of your expenses. Frank may follow you in a day or two—I'm not sure. Just now he's moving in with me.

GEORGIE. As crisp as lettuce, aren't you? (*She pauses and turns to Frank*) You want me to go back, Frank?

(FRANK *does not reply*)

(*After a pause*) That means yes. I'll go and pack. (*She moves to the door and turns*) But I want to know one thing: why do you hold on to this sack of trouble?

BERNIE (*coldly*) I will answer that, for Frank's sake. I'm interested in theatre, not show business. I could make a fortune in films, but that's show "biz" to me.

GEORGIE. What do you call this play, Literature?

BERNIE. That's true: it's show business, trying hard to be Theatre. And a man like Elgin, giving his best performance— he has the magic to transform a mere show to Theatre with a capital T.

GEORGIE (*quietly*) Let us hope. (*With a sad smile she turns to the door*)

BERNIE (*moving quickly to Georgie and detaining her*) One moment. Tell Frank he has nothing to worry about.

(GEORGIE *looks astonished and puzzled*)

He thinks you may go drastic. It's happened before, I understand.

FRANK (*putting his glass on the floor; murmuring nervously*) Bernie . . .

GEORGIE. What's happened before?

BERNIE. Phoney suicide attempts.

FRANK (*nervously*) Bernie, she wants to help.

GEORGIE (*closing her eyes; wearily*) Mr Dodd—we had a town idiot when I was a child—he kept insisting that elephant's tusks come from piano keys. You are very obtuse and wilful, for a man who so relishes his own humanity.

BERNIE. What are you talking about?

FRANK (*weakly*) Bernie, she has to pack . . .

BERNIE. What are you trying to tell me, Mrs Dodd?

GEORGIE. Don't call me Mrs Dodd. Suicide attempts are Frank's department.

BERNIE (*moving to Frank*) Show me your wrists, Frank. (*He pauses*) Show me your wrists. (*He pauses. Loudly*) I asked you to show me your wrists.

(FRANK, *agonized, slowly raises his wrists.* BERNIE *looks down at them for several intense seconds and the story is plain. Sickened,* BERNIE *turns and moves* R. GEORGIE, *standing by the door, averts her face.* FRANK'S *head slips down into his hands and he sobs without control.* BERNIE *slowly turns and looks at Georgie*)

I must ask you several questions.

GEORGIE (*moving to the trunk and leaning on it*) Michael on angel wings couldn't talk to me with your face.

BERNIE (*after a pause*) Frank may have to go back with you, unless you answer. He's been lying to me . . .

GEORGIE. He's incapable of the truth, as commonly understood.

BERNIE. You were "Miss America" in the late thirties?

GEORGIE. He told you that? (*She pauses and thinks for a moment*) Did—I burn down a house in Great Neck? Or a hotel suite? Did I need a nurse to watch me while he was tending work?

BERNIE (*nodding*) Umm.

GEORGIE. You didn't recognize any of it from the play you admired him in, *Werba's Millions*?

(FRANK *continues to sit with his hands to his face*)

(*Her eyes wet with tears, she talks on, spent, scarcely knowing what she is saying*) You don't know what it is—meet, marry, elope—nineteen, real cute, raised on too many books. Oh, my, I had such a naïve belief in Frank's wordliness and competence. (*She pauses*) Yes, I saw he drank—but that was only a pathetic hint of frailty in a wonderful glowing man. It was touching and sweet—it made me love him more. He could reform—I'd do it for him. Well, finally—there wasn't much to take over. (*She pauses and turns away*) Send him back to the hotel—he needs some rest. (*She takes a handkerchief from her handbag and dabs her nose*)

(BERNIE *hesitates a moment then crosses briskly to the door and opens it*)

BERNIE (*calling*) Larry.

(LARRY *enters immediately*)

LARRY. Yes, Bernie?

BERNIE. Is Ford out there? Is he "up" in Judge Murray's part?

LARRY. Yes, he is.

Bernie. Could he go on tonight?
Larry (*hesitantly*) Yes, I think he could.
Bernie (*murmuring thoughtfully*) Dunno what I'll do.
Frank (*gazing at the floor*) I'll play if I get another chance.

(Bernie's *face tightens*)

Bernie (*with a vicious jab of his thumb; harshly*) Take him back to the hotel. (*He turns and crosses to* r) Dismiss the company—check with me around five.
Larry (*crossing to the clothes hooks and taking down Frank's coat*) Yes, sir, Bernie.

(Frank *rises slowly and looks at Georgie*)

Georgie (*with her back to Frank; quietly*) Go on, Frank. I won't leave without seeing you.

(Frank *takes his coat from Larry, crosses and exits.* Larry *follows him off, closing the door. There is a silence.* Bernie *is tense and tender, smarting and apologetic.* Georgie *is abstracted and drained*)

Bernie (*presently*) May I smoke? (*He takes a cigarette from the box on the dressing-table*)
Georgie. May you smoke? What is that, homage to a lady? That will never make me forgive you, Mr Dodd, for what you've said and done.

(*There is a silence.* Bernie *does not look at Georgie, neither does he light his cigarette*)

Bernie. I'm very confused and troubled. What about Frank?
Georgie. Those lies are his big, respectable reason for having gone to pieces.
Bernie (*turning and moving* RC) Why did he go to pieces?
Georgie. It needs an Einstein to tell you that.
Bernie. I don't know where to begin apologizing, Mrs Dodd.
Georgie. I'm a real lemon drop. You can begin by not calling me Mrs Dodd. (*She flicks him a look and begins buttoning her coat*)
Bernie. Have you ever left him?
Georgie. Twice left, twice returned. He's a helpless child. (*She lifts her bag. Wryly*) Anyone taking a cab to New York?
Bernie (*with a step towards her*) But if he's as helpless as you say . . .
Georgie. He's not helpless now—he has you.
Bernie (*earnestly, his voice quivering*) Listen, he had to be watched and handled. You can do that—no-one else—I didn't know it before.
Georgie (*bitterly*) Then you've learned something—ripeness is all.
Bernie. Listen, Georgie, if . . .

GEORGIE (*opening up*) I don't intend to stay. (*She moves to the door*) Even the cat's dragged me up and down the stairs in this theatre.

BERNIE (*unhappily*) But the man needs you—he has to be watched.

GEORGIE (*turning; furiously angry*) *You* take on the job with waving banners and twelve hours later hand it back? *You're telling me!* (*She throws her bag on to the sofa and begins circling him*)

(BERNIE, *helpless, makes an attempt here and there to stop her torrential anger*)

Yes, he has to be watched—he has to be nursed, guarded and coddled. But not by me, my very young friend!

BERNIE. Please . . .

GEORGIE. I'm going back to New York, to the fiesta of a quiet room. For the first time in twelve years I won't have to wonder where he is—he'll be in the strong, sober hands of Mr Bernie Dodd!

BERNIE (*ineffectually*) Georgie, listen . . .

GEORGIE (*moving to* L *of Bernie*) Can you stand him up on his feet? Because that's where all my prayers have gone—to see that one holy hour when he can stand alone.

(BERNIE *tries to grab her*)

(*She avoids him*) And I might forgive even *you*, Mr Dodd, if you can keep him up long enough for me to get out from under. (*She moves* R) All I want is my own name and a modest job to buy the sugar for my coffee.

BERNIE (*moving towards Georgie, his temper slipping*) Wait—if you'll listen . . .

GEORGIE (*evading him and crossing to* LC) You can't believe that, can you, you goddam man? You can't believe a woman's crazy-out-of-her-mind to live alone. In one room. By herself.

(BERNIE, *aroused, grabs her by one arm.* GEORGIE *pulls away, but he grabs her with his other hand and whirls her around*)

BERNIE. Dammit, listen to me. You're knocking all the apologies out of my head. (*He pulls her in close to him and holds her by both arms*) Now, *listen*, Lady Brilliance: you have to stay—he doesn't play unless you stay. It's a time for promotion, not more execution. But I can't take the chance *if you don't stay!*

(*A quick tense moment follows,* GEORGIE *frozen in his arms, her hands against his chest*)

GEORGIE. Why are you holding me? (*She tries to free herself*) I said you are holding me.

(BERNIE *abruptly kisses her fully on the mouth, then they both step apart, and after a moment* BERNIE *sits on the sofa, turned from her, one hand up to his face*)

(*Thinly*) I . . . (*She seems to come out of a sleep*) What is that toughness of yours? A pose?

(BERNIE *puts his hand over his eyes; it is some time before he can trust himself to speak*)

To be so mad at someone you didn't even know. (*She pauses*) No-one has looked at me as a woman for years and years.

(BERNIE, *scowling, turns abruptly and faces her*)

You want to beat me up again, don't you?

BERNIE. No, I deserve anything you say—no excuses, no excuses. (*His manner changes*) Now I need your answer. For Frank's sake, I want you to stay.

GEORGIE. Wanting, wanting, always wanting.

BERNIE (*humbly*) I'm asking . . .

(*There is a tap at the door, then* COOK *enters briskly*)

COOK (*irritably*) Where are you, Bernie? I'm waiting. Ray Norton is on the phone—he's available. He can catch the sleeper and be here in the morning.

BERNIE. I'll be right there.

COOK. He's on the box-office phone.

BERNIE (*rising; sharply*) I'll be right there.

(COOK *glowers then exits quickly, slamming the door behind him*)

I have to go out now and battle him. He's armed with plenty of facts and weapons. Will you stay?

GEORGIE (*after a pause*) Yes.

(BERNIE, *his face rigid, crosses to the door*)

You kissed me—don't let it give you any ideas, Mr Dodd.

BERNIE (*quietly*) No, Mrs Elgin.

BERNIE *exits, quietly closing the door.* GEORGIE *stands for a full moment, as if listening, an air of impenetrable unreality about her. Her hand slowly moves up to her face. Her fingers touch her lips as—*

the CURTAIN *slowly falls*

E

To face page 66—Winter Journey

SCENE 3

SCENE—*A dressing-room in a New York Theatre. Some weeks later. Evening.*

The dressing-room opens directly on to the stage and part of the wall R is cut away so that part of the scenery of the play in which Frank is appearing can be seen. The room is attractive, comfortable and well-furnished. The door to the stage is in an alcove up R. There is a door L of the back wall leading to the bathroom. When the door is open, the wash-basin on the far wall can be seen. There is a dressing-table, a wardrobe, a sofa, three chairs and an occasional table. Frank's trunk stands L of the bathroom door. The alcove is furnished with a small table and a hat-stand.

(See the Ground Plan and Photograph of the Scene)

When the CURTAIN *rises, it is nearing the end of the second act of the play at its New York opening. From time to time stretches of dialogue can be heard from the play, and later, when the curtain drops, we will hear the applause. There is a hushed, tip-toe quality about everything. The door to the stage is open and* GEORGIE *is standing by it, listening to the play.* RALPH, *Frank's dresser, enters. He carries Frank's smoking jacket and several telegrams.*

RALPH. Excuse me. A few more telegrams. (*He hands the telegrams to Georgie, then crosses and hangs the jacket in the wardrobe*)

GEORGIE. Thanks. How is it going on the other side of the stage?

RALPH. A great guy, Mrs Elgin, he's a great guy. (*He goes into the bathroom, takes the towel from the rail, then comes back into the room*) Sure is a real experience to be working for him.

(GEORGIE *smiles.*

RALPH *exits, taking the towel with him.* GEORGIE *leafs through the telegrams, crosses to the dressing-table, picks up her spectacles and puts them on. One telegram interests her.*

BERNIE *enters. He is tense and nervous, all ears for the stage. He is in a strange and complex mood of cynicism and gloom, begrudging but not without hope, nervous and painful, with a quality of "riding" every-one and everything. He removes his coat and hangs it on the hat-stand.* GEORGIE, *startled, turns*)

GEORGIE. Where've you been, Bernie, out front?

BERNIE. Out front. On an opening night, the world's most useless man.

GEORGIE. How is Frank?

BERNIE (*admitting nothing*) His first act wasn't bad. How's it been back here?

GEORGIE. Quiet. Mr Cook came back but I wouldn't let him in. (*She opens the remaining telegrams and moves* C)

Bernie. More telegrams?

Georgie. This one is from Mr Unger's aunt.

Bernie (*moving down* r) Why don't you go out front?

Georgie. On a New York opening night? Not me, I don't sit out there with all those nabobs and critics. I hear very well right from here.

Bernie. That's the advantage of an on-stage dressing-room.

(Larry *appears in the doorway, a fierce working tool in shirt sleeves, minus his usual deference*)

Larry. Shh! Shh! Please! Quiet, dammit! Shh! There's a show going on.

(Larry *goes without concession, closing the door.* Bernie *sits down* r)

Georgie (*grimacing*) That's the *dis*advantage. (*Worried*) Isn't Frank's performance pleasing you?

Bernie (*annoyed*) He's erratic, in and out—the bursts aren't coming. We'll see.

Georgie (*crossing to the dressing-table*) Don't let him see your long face when he comes off. (*She puts the telegrams on the dressing-table*)

Bernie (*with a mock bow*) State Department Sadie—I forgot.

Georgie. Depressed, aren't you?

Bernie (*readily agreeing*) Depressed and mean. (*He sighs*) Well, it's been a long nine weeks. A job is a home to a homeless man. Now the job is finished—where do I go from here? (*Wryly*) I'm told—it has been intimated to me—that you call me Bernardo the Great.

Georgie (*crossing to Bernie*) Haven't you been a magician to Frank? To both of us, in fact?

Bernie (*rising and crossing impatiently to the hat-stand*) He can thank you for anything that's happened.

Georgie (*sincerely*) No, he can thank you, Bernie.

Bernie (*sourly*) Here we go, jockeying for position again. (*He turns. Abruptly tense*) Georgie, five weeks ago I kissed a woman, a married woman; and now I love a woman, a married woman, and don't know where to turn. (*He moves to Georgie, and holds her arms, his voice ardent but low*) Lady, lady, close to you this way . . .

Georgie (*gently*) Bernie . . .

Bernie. Who knows what'll happen after tonight—rehearsals are over—I may never see you again.

Georgie (*holding him off with her hands to his chest*) Bernie . . .

Bernie (*releasing her and smiling wryly*) Okay. (*He nervously snaps his fingers*) I didn't say before, what this must mean to you. No matter what happens to this show tonight—he'll have offers galore. (*He pauses*) Are you leaving him?

Georgie (*quietly*) Don't you think the subject can wait?

BERNIE (*with abrupt flare*) No, it happens to be on my mind. You've been evading me for weeks.

GEORGIE. You're unregenerate, Bernie—you'll never change. In a minute we'll be at each other's throats.

(GEORGIE *has not spoken unkindly, but* BERNIE, *it would seem, is ready to push to a fight*)

BERNIE. I don't mind a fight about something real. You could be a home for me—that's real. (*He abruptly lapses into gloom and sits on the chair up* C)

(FRANK'S *voice is heard lifted in a scene*)

Excuse me for blowing my wig. I can't escape that voice tonight— it follows me everywhere I go. (*He smirks*) Listen to him—he's ready to give that dark sterling silver quality to the best available parts. He needs you, dear.

GEORGIE. You're Frank's friend—you're thinking of his future —I like that. But what about mine?

BERNIE (*rising; gloomily*) Right, right, only right—I can't tell you what to do, can I? But how can a man be so disgruntled and still live? (*With his face averted he runs a nervous hand through his hair*)

GEORGIE (*moving sympathetically to him*) I hate to see you this way, troubled, contrite.

BERNIE (*harshly*) Lecture me no lectures.

GEORGIE. Now, why don't you stop clenching your fists to hide your tenderness and pity? (*She smiles*) Put your eyes down before they burn a hole in me.

BERNIE (*staring at her*) Are you leaving him?

GEORGIE. Don't be wilful, dear. You see, you'll go on . . .

(*She breaks off as* BERNIE *abruptly turns his head and listens sharply to the stage play. He bounds to the door and opens it, ears even bigger.* GEORGIE *moves to Bernie, not knowing what is wrong. The sound of running feet and excited whispers are heard off.* FRANK'S *voice has risen high, bellowing and angry.*

NANCY *appears in the doorway. She is excited and half hysterical.* BERNIE *brings her into the room.* RALPH *appears in the doorway, waiting for orders*)

BERNIE (*leading* NANCY *to the chair* R; *impatiently*) Shh, quiet! What happened? Shh!

NANCY (*sobbing*) He began to hit me, Bernie—on stage. (*She sits*) I can't bear it! I don't know what he's doing out there— he's even changed the lines.

BERNIE (*mordant and cutting*) Quiet, quiet, this is an opening night. (*He turns to Ralph. Harshly*) Close the door, Ralph—get back to your job.

(RALPH *exits and closes the door*)

NANCY (*excitedly*) He's—he's—his eyes are red—he looks right at you and doesn't see you. He's—I began to cry—he took me and shook me like a doll.

BERNIE (*sharply*) Come on now, it didn't hurt that much. That's the scene.

NANCY. To shake me and slap me like that? And to change the lines? I didn't know what to answer him.

BERNIE. Don't raise your voice—the curtain is up.

(NANCY *sullenly rubs her smarting face*)

GEORGIE (*crossing to Nancy*) Are you all right, dear?

NANCY. Yes, I'm all right, Mrs Elgin—I'm all right.

BERNIE. Now stop sulking, Junior Miss—go up and change for your last act.

NANCY (*rising*) Yes, I will, Bernie, I will—it was just such a shock, Mrs Elgin.

BERNIE. I hope that's the biggest shock you ever get. Go on, now.

(NANCY, *wary of Bernie's mood, crosses to the door*)

(*He moves* C) Come here.

NANCY (*turning*) Me?

BERNIE. Come here.

(NANCY *moves slowly to* BERNIE, *who unbends and unsmilingly kisses her. She is happy again*)

Go up and change.

NANCY. Yes, I will, Bernie, yes—gee . . .

(NANCY *exits. Scowling,* BERNIE *goes to the door and looks out.* GEORGIE *follows Bernie to the door*)

GEORGIE. It was spooky—he's wild out there—he almost knocked her down.

BERNIE (*impatiently*) I've been waiting *forty minutes* for that burst! If he can play scenes like that, let him do what he wants.

(*They stand listening at the door.* FRANK'S *voice can be heard*)

(*After a pause*) Here comes the curtain.

(*Out of sight, the curtain has come down on the Second Act. The applause is strong. The sounds of swarming stagehands are heard.* BERNIE *and* GEORGIE *step aside.*

FRANK *enters like a man in a perspiring trance, heavy and hoarse, keyed into the just completed scene. He is breathing heavily, like a boxer between two late rounds.*

RALPH *follows Frank on. He carries Frank's overcoat, hat and stick*)

FRANK. Close that window.

(BERNIE *takes the coat, hat and stick from Ralph*)

GEORGIE. There's no window in here.

(BERNIE *waves Ralph away.*
RALPH *exits, closing the door behind him*)

FRANK (*moving down* L) I'm dripping wet. (*He removes his coat*)
GEORGIE (*crossing to* R *of Frank; warily*) Get your clothes off.

(FRANK *throws off Georgie's attentions with a lifted arm and, half sobbing, waves an embittered fist at the world*)

FRANK. I couldn't hold myself back. Belted, belted! Did I hurt the kid?

(BERNIE *puts the coat, hat and stick on the chair up* C)

(*He turns to Bernie*) Bernie, I couldn't help it, Bernie. I started to go and I couldn't help it.

BERNIE (*attempting to lead* FRANK *to the chair* L) Sit down and take it easy.

GEORGIE. Sit down, Frank, sit down.

FRANK. I'm sorry, kid, forgive me—it just came out that way. That's what he should do there, the Judge—no-one wants him, not even his grandchild. And suddenly I got the image—they're caging a lion—like you shove him in the face. Like they do in the circus, with chairs and brooms. And I couldn't hold it back. (*He sits on the sofa*)

BERNIE (*firmly*) I didn't want you to hold it back.

GEORGIE. Now get your jacket off. (*Standing behind Frank, she peels off his dinner jacket and hangs it in the wardrobe*)

(*Intermission music is heard off*)

FRANK (*removing his collar and tie*) This is limp—I'll need a fresh one. (*He hands the collar to Georgie*)

(GEORGIE *puts the collar on the trunk and gets out a clean one*)

I hope I didn't hurt that kid.

BERNIE (*moving down* R) Don't worry—she's fine.

FRANK (*sighing; relieved*) Well, nobody's sore at nobody then. Golly, I was wild out there for a minute. (*He rises and crosses to Bernie*) They made me sore out front, too—they're sitting on their hands.

BERNIE (*mordantly*) They may be very moved.

FRANK (*growling but pleased*) Don't kid the ugly man.

BERNIE (*soberly*) I'm not kidding—your performance can only be a big surprise.

FRANK. That's swell! I hope so. (*He crosses to the dressing-table*) Say, did you see that hospital scene? She's good, that Mabel Beck. (*He picks up the telegrams from the dressing-table, and turns*) Here are some more wires. Someone must remember Poppa. Here's one from Sue Lewis. ". . . renewal of a great career. Am out front rooting. Much affection and regards . . ." (*The wire seems to affect him in a strange way. He looks furtively at Georgie with something on his mind. Briskly*) Let's see—what am I wearing next?

GEORGIE (*moving to the wardrobe*) The smoking jacket, dear. (*She takes the jacket from the wardrobe*)

FRANK (*to Bernie*) Jo-jo, the dog-faced boy—I wish I had four hands. Well, as long as you excused me for going wild . . .

BERNIE (*crossing to the door*) Keep going wild and I'll bless you in Macy's window.

(COOK *enters. He is wearing a hat which he does not remove*)

Here's Philip Cook, Esquire—he'll do *even more* than I will in Macy's window. Be back.

(BERNIE *exits*)

FRANK. How is it out front, Mr Cook? (*He pours himself a glass of milk from the bottle on the dressing-table*)

COOK. I only know what I read in the papers. How do you feel?

FRANK (*sitting at the dressing-table*) Good, good—pluperfect good. (*He sips his milk*)

COOK. The reactions in the lobby are pretty good. You hungry?

FRANK (*indicating the glass*) This? It's for my voice.

COOK (*moving down* R; *uneasily*) Frank, a lot of things—are said in the heat and toil of the day. I hope you'll accept my apologies.

FRANK. Sure, we all know how those things can happen. (*He has a sudden thought and turns in his chair*) Of course, you include my wife, too, in your apologies.

COOK (*quickly*) Of course, Mrs Elgin, I include you, too—of course.

FRANK. Then start by taking your hat off—you're not at a smoker, Mr Cook.

(COOK *is very thrown by this attitude.* GEORGIE *silently watches the scene*)

This is the first polite word you've had for either one of us. And I think I know why. You . . .

COOK (*moving up* C) Frank, it's human—if we have to protect a show—naturally . . .

FRANK. You want me to sign a run-of-the-play contract before the morning papers are out, for half of what I'm worth. Isn't that about it, Cookie?

COOK (*after a pause; removing his hat*) I'm really very sorry, Frank, and you have to believe me on a thing like that. As to different contractual arrangements—it *was* on my mind.

(Cook *bows stiffly and slithers sideways out of the room*)

FRANK. I guess *that* put a pimple on his nose. (*Alarmed*) I hope I didn't say too much.

GEORGIE (*laughing*) He thinks you're wonderful in the show, but he wouldn't have the grace to say so. Just you keep your self-respect, the way you have it out on that stage tonight. (*She moves to him with the smoking jacket*)

(FRANK *rises*)

And remember, Frank, don't forget—it isn't necessary to be liked by every Tom, Dick and Harry Truman, even if he's president.

(GEORGIE *assists* FRANK *to put on the smoking jacket.* FRANK *hums his favourite little tune*)

FRANK. You're a real scrapper—I've always admired your nerve.

GEORGIE. Still some shine on your face.

FRANK (*sitting at the dressing-table*) I'll fix it. (*He powders. Thoughtfully*) That was nice of Sue, that wire.

GEORGIE (*levelly*) Yes, it was. (*She pauses*) You're handsome tonight.

FRANK (*rising slowly and turning*) Am I? (*Seriously*) Well, after tonight—catch this one and tuck it in your memory book—you'll never again have to ask why you married me.

GEORGIE (*putting a handkerchief in Frank's breast pocket; quietly*) Won't I?

(*A serious moment is about to take place, but it is broken by a tap on the door.*
BERNIE *enters.* FRANK *picks up his collar*)

BERNIE (*crossing to the chair* R) Friend Mabel sends her love. (*He sits*)

(GEORGIE *sits on the sofa*)

FRANK (*abruptly*) Don't wanna be a pest, kid, but can I show you something? No collar and tie—just a collar button.

BERNIE. You mean go on that way?

FRANK. Yes, that's the way they arrest him, without a collar—from collar button to collar button in thirty years. Get it?

BERNIE (*half smiling*) It's a real point—leave it in.

(RALPH *appears in the doorway*)

RALPH. They're ready, Mr Elgin.

(RALPH *exits.*
FRANK *picks up a telegram and fingers it as he looks at himself in the mirror*)

LARRY (*off; calling*) Places, places. Third Act, please. Places.

(LARRY *appears in the doorway*)

You ready, Frank?

(BERNIE *rises and crosses to the door*)

FRANK (*without turning*) Yes, thanks, kid, all ready.

BERNIE (*grabbing Larry by the arm*) Larry, don't take the curtain up till they're all seated—the front rows in particular.

LARRY (*grinning*) If the front rows had the balcony's manners—what a world this could be.

(LARRY *exits. His third act cry is heard as a distant echo for quite some time*)

FRANK (*turning; with hesitant nervousness*) Georgie—I can be wrong most of the time—but any ideas you have, if you want to leave me—don't.

(BERNIE *is about to leave, but* FRANK *stops him by crossing to him*)

I'm deliberately talking in front of a third person. Maybe I should do it more often—sometimes it's a big relief to fall on your face in public. (*He crosses to Georgie*) Am I wrong, Georgie? Aren't you setting up Sue Lewis to put in your place? (*He sits on the sofa and faces her*) Don't leave me, darling. Give me a chance. I love you.

(GEORGIE *pauses for her answer; one of her hands creeps up to the lapel of Frank's coat*)

GEORGIE. Frank, I certainly didn't want to bring up any of this tonight. But you did—so let's have the whole truth. I married you for happiness, Frank—and, if necessary, I'll leave you for the same reason. Right now I don't know where I stand.

FRANK (*humbly*) You don't?

GEORGIE (*dropping her hand and carefully picking her way*) No. Because neither of us has really changed. And yet I'm sure that both our lives are at some sort of turning point—there's some real new element of hope here—I don't know what. But I'm uncertain—and you, Frank, have to be strong enough to bear that uncertainty.

FRANK (*hushed*) I think I know what you mean.

(LARRY *enters*)

LARRY. We're waiting, Frank.

(LARRY *exits*)

FRANK (*rising; nervously*) They're waiting, dear.

(GEORGIE *rises*)

I—I don't know how to say this—but no matter what happens, you have saved me, Georgie—you and Bernie. (*He kisses her and pulls himself together*) I think I have a chance.

(FRANK *turns, crosses and exits firmly. After a moment,* BERNIE *seems about to say something to* GEORGIE, *but she is moved and withdrawn*)

BERNIE (*muttering*) I'd better show my face on stage a moment —rah-rah stuff.

(BERNIE *exits.*
PAUL *enters, almost brushing Bernie.* PAUL *wears dinner clothes*)

PAUL (*crossing to Georgie; jubilantly*) Frank is magnificent. He's really showing me what my play is all about.
GEORGIE (*smiling*) He's on stage—they're going up.
PAUL. You don't look like a veteran of all the wars tonight. You must be damn proud. I know my aunt is—we're sitting together. She's showing all the proprietary interest of a mother hen.
GEORGIE (*quietly*) Give your aunt my regards.
PAUL. I will.

(PAUL *moves sweetly close to Georgie, wanting to kiss her or touch her hands. She attempts the same, but it is clumsy and fizzles out.*
PAUL *turns, crosses and exits.* GEORGIE *slowly moves to the door; she is thoughtful and inward as she looks out.*
BERNIE *enters, his spirits slightly lifted. The intermission music dies away*)

LARRY (*off; calling cautiously*) Quiet backstage, please, we're going up—quiet, please.
BERNIE (*glancing over his shoulder*) He's so excited. (*To Georgie*) Everything ship-shape.
GEORGIE (*after a pause*) It was sweet of you to send him all hose wires.
BERNIE (*impassively*) Who told you?
GEORGIE. Guessed. How many did you send?
BERNIE. Nine or ten. And you?
GEORGIE. Four or five.
LARRY (*off; calling*) Quiet, everybody. Curtain going up.
BERNIE. There she goes.

(*The curtain has gone up.* GEORGIE *and* BERNIE *are looking out. A strained pause is followed by a rumble of applause*)

(*Mordantly*) Applauding a third act entrance—surprise follows surprise. (*He moves down* R) Well, this is the act where he wraps up the show and walks off with the town.
GEORGIE (*leaning against the door jamb; to herself*) He's handsome tonight. (*She turns and crosses to* L)
BERNIE. I'll go out front and watch. Good night, Georgie. (*He crosses to* R *of her*)
GEORGIE. He'll come off dripping again.

(*She hums a snatch of Frank's tune. When she turns* BERNIE *has moved in closer to her, almost forcibly making her aware of his presence*)

BERNIE. Good night, Georgie.

(*They are face to face*)

GEORGIE (*gently*) Good night, Bernardo.

BERNIE (*wryly*) I don't know—maybe a magician does live in this frail, foolish body, but he certainly can't work wonders for himself. (*He fishes in his pocket*) You'll never leave him. (*He jerks his hand almost angrily from his pocket*) I keep running out of cigarettes.

GEORGIE (*gently*) You smoke too much.

BERNIE (*mockingly*) You are impertinent, madame. (*Longingly*) And steadfast. And loyal—reliable. I like that in a woman.

GEORGIE (*putting a hand on his arm*) Wrestle, Bernie—you may win a blessing. But stay unregenerate. Life knocks the sauciness out of us soon enough.

BERNIE, *lonely, arch and rueful, looks at Georgie for a moment before stepping in and kissing her lightly on the lips. Then he turns, crosses, takes his overcoat from the stand and slowly exits. For a moment* GEORGIE *wears a sad and yearning look, then recalls herself to reality. She takes Frank's robe from the wardrobe and moves towards the door. Meanwhile Frank's stage voice is heard, playing a quiet but powerful scene. A thought makes* GEORGIE *stop. She goes back to the dressing-table, picks up a telegram, considers it quickly, comes to a decision, crumples the telegram into a ball and throws it into the waste-paper basket. Then, head up, with Frank's robe across her arm, she crosses and slowly exits as—*

the CURTAIN *slowly falls*

FURNITURE AND PROPERTY PLOT

ACT I

SCENE 1

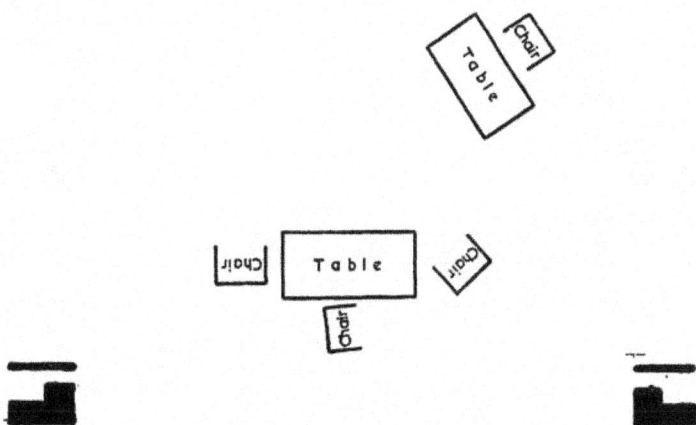

On stage—Producer's table. *On it:* prompt script in cover, script for Paul,
                    part—Judge Murray, clock, ashtray
      Table up L. *On it:* telephone, ashtray, script
      4 chairs
      Bench. *On it:* Nancy's part, Paul's brief-case
      Bucket (LC)
      Packs of scenery
      Spot and floodlights
      Electrician's ladder
Personal— FRANK: cigarettes, matches, newspaper, 2 parts
      COOK: cigar, matches
      PAUL: notebook, pencil
      BERNIE: chewing gum
other furniture and equipment as required to dress the stage.

SCENE 2

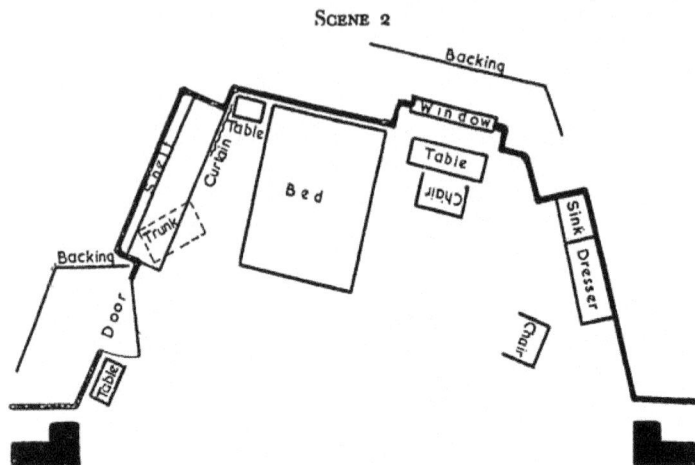

On stage—Table (down R) *On it:* radio. *Under it:* books
Frank's photograph (*on wall above radio*)
Hanging on door: pyjamas, dressing-gown
In recess: cabin trunk (open), shaving mirror on wall
On hooks: Frank's jacket and tie, dresses
 On shelf above recess: shirts, clothes, shaving mug, talcum powder,
    shaving lotion, 2 suitcases, brush and comb
 Table (up R) *On it:* clock, photograph, cigarettes, matches, ashtray
 Bed. *On it:* mattress, bedspread, suitcase (half packed) Georgie's
   clothes for packing
 Table (in window) *On it:* tablecloth, books, lamp, clock
 Hanging on bedpost: Georgie's blouse
 On floor L of bed: Frank's slippers
 On window sill: bottle of milk
 Sink. *Under it:* bucket, washing-up bowl, teacloth
 Dresser. *On it:* cups, saucers, milk jug, sugar, bottle of hand lotion,
   plates, clock, stove, toaster, coffee tin
   On stove: percolator with coffee
 2 chairs
 Window curtains
 Rugs on floor
 2 pairs wall brackets (imitation gas)
Personal— BERNIE: notebook and pencil, watch, cigarettes, lighter, $20 bill
 FRANK: newspaper
 GEORGIE: spectacles

SCENE 3

Set as for Act 1, Scene 1
Set—*On Producer's table:* prompt script in cover, ashtray (full), 2 coffee mugs
 (empty)
 On floor under table: bucket, sandwich papers
 On table up L: Judge's part, telephone, ashtray (full), blotter, inkstand,
 empty coffee mug, script
 On bench: newspapers, sandwich papers, Larry's coat, Nancy's coat and part
 On chair R: Bernie's coat
 On chair L: Frank's coat and hat
Personal—BERNIE: cigarettes, lighter

SCENE 4

Set as for Act 1, Scene 2

Set—Window table down L. *On it:* white tablecloth, 2 plates, 2 knives, 2 each
cups, saucers, teaspoons, 2 grapefruit spoons,
newspapers

On door: Frank's overcoat. *In pocket:* part and address book

In recess: Frank's jacket and tie

On shelf: talcum powder, shaving lotion, laundry parcel containing clean
shirt, Frank's hat

On trunk: coins, handkerchief

On table up R: open book, Georgie's spectacles, newspaper

On bed (rumpled): pyjamas

On floor R: Frank's slippers

Under sink: work-basket with needle and thread

On stove: percolator with coffee, kettle

On bedposts: soiled shirt, towel

On floor by sink: 2 empty beer bottles

In sink: shaving mug, razor, mirror

On dresser: 2 dishes grapefruit

SCENE 5

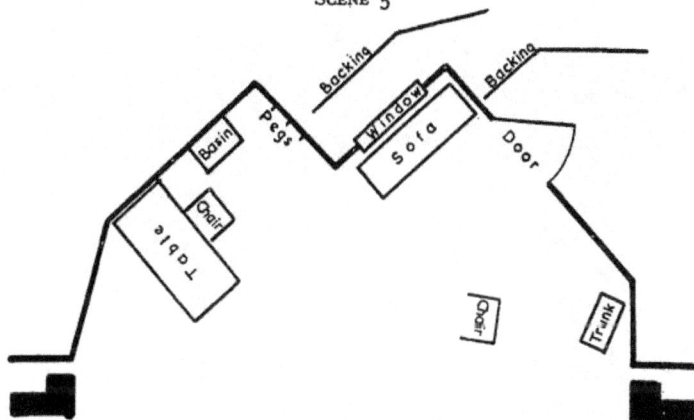

On stage—Dressing-table. *On it:* box with cigarettes, matches, box of tissues,
tin of powder, hair brush, comb, remover cream,
wig block, make-up materials, towel, ashtray, part
(Judge Murray), small mirror, cotton wool
Under it: wig boxes

Waste-paper basket

Chair (R) *On it:* towel, Frank's street trousers

Tall cheval mirror

Wash-basin. *In it:* soap, face flannel, mug of fresh water

Sofa. *On it:* newspaper, costume shirt

Chair (LC) *On it:* Frank's tie

Cabin trunk (open) *In it:* disarranged clothing
On it: radio, knitting in bag

On clothes pegs: dressing-gown, smoking jacket, street shirt, street
jacket, costume coat

On floor under pegs: Frank's shoes

On shelf: hat-box

On corner shelf: electric fan

On shelf behind basin: clothes brush, ashtray, nailbrush

Personal— GEORGIE: handbag. *In it:* aspirins, chewing gum, spectacles, lipstick,
powder compact

LARRY: script
PAUL: typewriter, brief-case, script
BERNIE: packet with one cigarette, lighter, script
FRANK: part

ACT II

SCENE 1

Set as previous scene
Set—On dressing-table: bottle of cough syrup (half filled) empty coffee mug, 3
    fan letters
    On sofa: newspapers, Paul's briefcase, typewriter, jacket, overcoat, script
    On chair LC: Georgie's knitting, handbag and coat
    Down R: Frank's shoes
    On trunk: newspaper cuttings, coffee mug (half full)
    In bottom drawer of trunk: full bottle of cough syrup
    In basin: mug of fresh water
Personal— GEORGIE: handkerchief, watch, chewing gum
        BERNIE: aspirins, notebook, pencil
        FRANK: cigarettes, matches

SCENE 2

Set as previous scene
Set—On floor below sofa: whisky bottle, Frank's hat
Off stage—Glass of alka-seltzer (GEORGIE)
Personal—LARRY: matches

SCENE 3

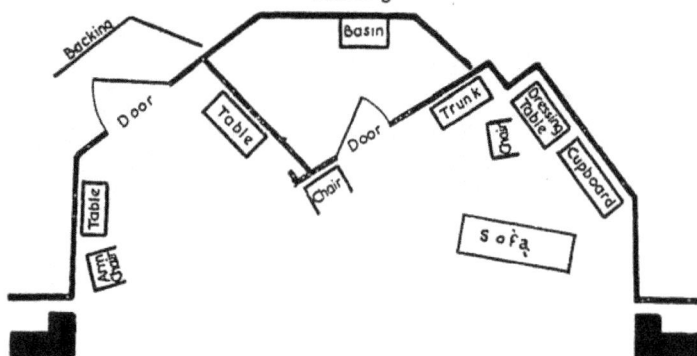

On stage—Reversed flats (R)
    Table (R) *On it:* lamp, ashtray
    Dressing-table. *On it:* materials as previous scene, plus bottle of milk,
          glass, Georgie's spectacles, handkerchief
    Waste-paper basket
    In bathroom: wash-basin, towel
    Wardrobe. *In it:* costume coat, dressing-gown
    Frank's trunk. *On it:* hat-box. *In it:* collar
    Table in alcove. *On it:* vase of flowers
             Over it: picture
    Hat-stand
    Sofa. *On it:* cushion
    3 chairs
    Curtain for alcove
    Carpet on floor
Off stage—Smoking jacket, telegrams (RALPH)
        Overcoat, hat and stick (RALPH)
Personal—GEORGIE: handbag. *In it:* handkerchief, lipstick, powder compact

LIGHTING PLOT

Property fittings required:
Act I	Scene 1	Pilot light
	Scene 2	2 wall brackets
	Scene 3	Pilot light
	Scene 4	2 wall brackets
	Scene 5	2 dressing-table lights
Act II	Scene 1	The same
	Scene 2	The same
	Scene 3	Table lamp, dressing-table lights

ACT I SCENE 1 A stage Interior. Morning
THE MAIN ACTING AREAS are round the table C, and the desk, up LC
THE APPARENT SOURCE OF LIGHT is from the working light
OFF STAGE LIGHTING: open floods shining from wings
To open: cold, gloomy light concentrated on C stage
No cues

ACT I SCENE 2 A furnished room
Interior. Morning
THE MAIN ACTING AREAS are by the door R, round the bed C, and by the table L
THE APPARENT SOURCE OF LIGHT is from the wall brackets L and R
OFF STAGE LIGHTING: dull grey light outside window; strip outside door
To open: dull, artificial light; brackets on
No cues

ACT I SCENE 3
To open: The same as for Act I Scene 1
Cue 1   BERNIE. . . . My wife wants money.   (Page 20)
    Switch off batten
Note: The pilot light switched on by LARRY (page 20) is worked by an independent switch

ACT I SCENE 4 The same as for Act I Scene 2

ACT I SCENE 5 A Boston theatre dressing-room
Interior. Night
THE MAIN ACTING AREAS are by the dressing table R, by the couch, up C, by the door LC, and round the chair LC
THE APPARENT SOURCE OF LIGHT is the theatre dressing-table lights
OFF STAGE LIGHTING: night sky outside window; strip outside door
To open: cold, artificial light; practicals on
No cues

ACT II SCENE 1 The same as for Act I Scene 5
Cue 2   FRANK switches off dressing-table lights   (Page 53)
    Take out lighting round dressing-table

ACT II SCENE 2 The same as for Act I Scene 5
OFF STAGE LIGHTING: glimmer of light outside window; strip outside door
To open: darkness
Cue 3   FRANK switches on dressing-table lights   (Page 57)
    Bring up lighting round dressing-table
Cue 4   BERNIE switches on room lights   (Page 59)
    Bring up remainder of lighting

ACT II SCENE 3 A New York theatre dressing-room
Interior. Evening
THE MAIN ACTING AREAS are by the door R, by the chair C, and round the dressing-table and couch L
THE APPARENT SOURCE OF LIGHT is from a table lamp R and from the dressing-table lights L
OFF STAGE LIGHTING: darkness
To open: bright, artificial light; practicals on
No cues